Tracking Respondents: A Multi-Method Approach

The Entry into Careers Series

Luther B. Otto, Series Editor
Boys Town Center
Boys Town, Nebraska

Tracking Respondents: A Multi-Method Approach

Volume II: Entry into Careers Series

Vaughn R.A. Call
Luther B. Otto
Kenneth I. Spenner
Boys Town Center

LexingtonBooks
D.C. Heath and Company
Lexington, Massachusetts
Toronto

Library of Congress Cataloging in Publication Data

Call, Vaughn R.A.
    Tracking respondents.

    (Entry into careers series; v. 2)
    Bibliography: p.
    Includes index.
    1. Panel analysis. 2. Occupational surveys. I. Otto, Luther B. II. Spenner,
Kenneth I. III. Title. IV. Series: Otto, Luther B. Entry into careers series; v. 2.
H61.C233   300'.724   81-48624
ISBN 0-669-03644-7   AACR2

Published simultaneously in Canada

Printed in the United States of America

International Standard Book Number: 0-669-03644-7

Library of Congress Catalog Card Number: 81-48624

To Kathryn and Nancy

Contents

List of Figures

List of Tables

Preface and Acknowledgments

This book explains how to locate participants in panel or follow-up studies. It outlines a tracking strategy that maximizes the number of panel members located and minimizes tracking costs. Although oriented toward large-scale, long-term tracking efforts, the principles and procedures can also be applied to smaller follow-up studies.

We had several types of readers in mind when we wrote this book. Researchers will find this book helpful in three ways. First, the Comprehensive Tracking Model we present provides a framework for developing a tracking strategy and may guide future research on the effectiveness and efficiency of tracking procedures. Second, the book summarizes a number of successful panel studies and informs researchers about what was done and how successful it was. Third, we present in considerable detail the development and execution of the tracking phase of the Career Development Study. We provide rules of thumb that assisted us in locating 98.1 percent of our 6,729 panel members twelve years after they were first studied.

We were also mindful of the interests of workers in organizations, who must locate current addresses for a large number of people. Hospitals, government agencies, businesses with employees in hazardous occupations, and alumni associations are examples. People who work for these organizations may not be researchers and may not have a background in the social sciences. Therefore, we included details and provided examples whenever we felt that a concept may not be familiar to some readers.

This book will be especially helpful to novice trackers. It presents details on how to identify and use information sources, suggests ways to contact a particular information source, and provides insights and solutions to problems that may occur during tracking.

This book supplements material commonly presented in methods textbooks and courses. Heavy emphasis is usually given to cross-sectional research procedures, but comments about panel studies are usually much more limited. We hope to interest students in learning more about survey methods in panel studies. This book, together with volume I in the series, provides new material on the process of conducting a panel study.

Our major objective is to begin to answer the question that confronts researchers planning a panel study: How does one find panel members so that a follow-up study can be successful? The question is common because locating respondents in panel studies is not given detailed attention in the literature. Unlike subjects for which a copious literature exists, the literature on tracking is sparse. Although numerous large panel studies have been completed successfully, the rationale and procedures remain archived

xiii

in project files or etched in the principal investigator's memory. The knowledge of problems encountered during tracking and solutions to those problems either became part of the research lore shared verbally with associates or was lost as projects turned to substantive analyses and experienced trackers took employment elsewhere. Although some information about tracking is shared and known, too often the details governing the efficient organization, operation, and execution of tracking efforts must be rediscovered with each new study.

Part of the reluctance of researchers to conduct panel studies is this lack of knowledge and experience with procedures for locating participants a few or sometimes many years after an initial study. The lack of a cumulative body of literature on tracking further compounds the problem of trying to devise a tracking strategy that fits the researcher's special needs.

We believe that this book marks an important point in the development of tracking procedures because it introduces a formal examination of the logic behind tracking. Part of the book's value lies in initiating an effort to systematize tracking into a set of propositions and processes that guide the location of panel members.

We have tried to write a comprehensive book. Nonetheless, we recognize that we have left many questions unanswered. However, the question concerning the possibility of locating respondents is answered. We demonstrate that it is possible to locate and reinterview most panel members in a large, long-term panel study. The challenge is to replace impressions and deductions based on experience with empirically supported propositions that aid researchers in making decisions about a tracking strategy. We hope this material provides a groundwork upon which other researchers can build.

As in any other large project, numerous people and organizations contributed to the success we enjoyed. Many who assisted in the day-to-day tasks are not mentioned here by name, but their excellent work is acknowledged and appreciated.

We are indebted to the Boys Town Center for the institutional support that made this book and our study possible. We also acknowledge the participation of the Social Research Center at Washington State University, James F. Short, Jr., director.

We thank David Chapin for designing innovative software that reduced tracking tasks from herculean efforts to simple routines, organized massive amounts of information into easy-to-access computer files, and produced thousands of personalized letters. We appreciate David's painstaking efforts to ensure that the software fit our needs. His friendship and interest in the project will not be forgotten.

Sandy Wendel contributed to this book in several ways. We particularly appreciate her efforts in tracking panel members from several schools that posed difficult tracking problems and her secretarial and copyediting assistance in preparing this manuscript for publication.

We were fortunate to have the services of a number of excellent trackers. Cynthia Evahn, Elisabeth Trembath, Judy Zucker, Susie Silverman, Mabel Zimmerman, and Emily Chapin were responsible for finding most of our hard-to-find respondents. We recognize Cynthia Evahn's special efforts, diligence, and initiative in supervising most of the tracking activity. Her attention to detail and willingness to go the extra mile greatly facilitated the day-to-day operation.

Success in tracking ultimately depends on the willingness of respondents and community members to help. We are indebted to the 6,729 participants who gave of their time to make the study a success. We give special recognition to the dozens of high-school reunion committee members who not only provided reunion address lists but also spent considerable time helping our trackers find their classmates.

Our tracking strategy required mailing thousands of personalized letters. The Boys Town mailing division efficiently produced and assembled those letters. Word processing at the Boys Town Center aided in the production of letters and prepared this manuscript. We thank Dorothy Runte, Mary Pat Roy, Marilyn Pittillo, and Donna Plaisted for their extra efforts and accommodation to our schedule.

The opinions expressed in this book do not necessarily reflect the position or policy of the Boys Town Center, and no endorsement should be inferred. Total responsibility for the content rests with, and is accepted by the authors.

**Tracking
Respondents:
A Multi-Method
Approach**

1 Introduction

The problem of finding people or locating their current addresses and telephone numbers is neither new nor novel. Every day thousands of people are the subject of searches. The search may be as simple as opening a telephone book, as inexpensive as mailing a letter, as complicated as filing a form with the bureau of missing persons, or as costly as hiring a private detective.

The problem of tracking groups of people in a highly mobile society can be substantial. Telephone books become dated before the ink dries and the book is bound. Mail travels routinely by jet but is forwarded by the postal service for only a short period of time. As time passes and memories fade, former neighbors, friends, and acquaintances lose contact. Credit agencies fail to find debtors, class-reunion booklets increasingly indicate "address unknown," inactive membership lists grow longer, inheritances go unclaimed, and research studies designed to restudy participants suffer because of lost cases.

How does the researcher find study participants who have not been contacted for several years? What approaches reestablish contact most successfully? How successful can one expect to be? How much will the effort cost? These are the questions researchers face, and these are the issues this book addresses.

Tracking as a Craft

The answers to these questions are elusive. Partial replies are published in research articles and supplementary documentation. Typically, more detailed and sometimes more helpful responses are hidden in unpublished reports and training manuals used in panel studies.

Over a decade ago Eckland (1968) observed that researchers contemplating panel designs have little technical information about how to find panel members other than their own experience, a few advisory articles, and the personally communicated dos and don'ts of their colleagues. The utility and importance of panel research for the study of change and causation has been recognized since Lazarsfeld's articles on panel research forty years ago (Lazarsfeld and Fiske 1938; Lazarsfeld 1948). Nonetheless, the methodological literature continues to be scarce, technique oriented, noncumulative, and largely inaccessible.

1

Given the importance of panel designs, why is the theoretical and methodological literature on tracking so poorly developed? There appear to be three reasons. First, although researchers may pose questions and, implicitly, develop hypotheses about the effectiveness of alternate tracking techniques, the expense and long-term nature of the tracking effort act as a damper on the prospect of conducting experimental studies on tracking. Few researchers are inclined to risk their limited panel members and resources on the uncertainties of a methodological experiment.

Second, details of tracking efforts are generally not provided in journal articles. Indeed, panel data are often reported as if they are cross-sectional data. As a result, readers cannot tell what tracking procedures were effective, and the writer generates little interest in the issue of tracking results.

Third, interested scholars have been content to concentrate on reviewing the tracking techniques used by others. A set of techniques, a bag of tracking tricks, has emerged from these summaries, and a research lore based on the experiences of panel researchers has developed that would have us believe that success is determined by the number and correct application of the tricks of the trade. The more tricks you know and the more you can do, the more past study participants you will find. That seems to be the message. As a result, tracking has become more of a craft than a science (Clarridge, Sheehy, and Hauser 1977). The occasional successes achieved in tracking have tempered the immediate need for further methodological advancements.

The problem with the craft orientation is that it does not tell why certain techniques work or under what conditions what techniques should be applied. The craft orientation lacks a theoretical rationale for human behavior that explains why people participate in follow-up studies. Rather than focus on what makes respondents tick, the craft orientation focuses on techniques—on what researchers do. If a technique does not produce the expected results, the outcomes are explained ex post facto in terms of the researcher's ingenuity, dedication, tenacity, and persistence—or the lack of these qualities. Instead of looking for underlying similarities and themes in successful tracking, the craft orientation retreats to the position that the project should have worked harder on tracking. The craft orientation focuses on techniques rather than on people. Therefore, it offers little guidance on how to structure a tracking strategy that assures the highest response in the shortest time for the lowest cost.

An Alternative Perspective

This book presents a different perspective on tracking. It focuses on the respondents rather than on tracking techniques. We refer to it as the *Com-*

prehensive Tracking Model. This model incorporates aspects of the craft orientation but is more than just tracking techniques. Tracking is viewed as a process that integrates a logic for why people respond with a method for organizing tracking techniques. What results is a design that outlines procedures for locating study participants.

The necessity for integrating theory and procedures lies in the nature of panel and follow-up studies. Panel and follow-up studies require the collection of data from the same people or groups of people at two or more points in time.[1] Under ideal circumstances, a researcher is able to track all panel members and to obtain the data required for all measurement periods, but that ideal is seldom obtained, and panel attrition occurs.

Panel attrition is the loss of study participants through nonresponse to second or subsequent measurements. Six major sources of nonresponse account for panel attrition:

1. Respondent's death;
2. Respondent's inability to participate;
3. Researcher's failure to locate respondent;
4. Researcher's inability to interview respondent;
5. Respondent's refusal to participate; and
6. Researcher's mismanagement of information.[2]

Respondent's death or severe physical or mental impairments are unanticipated events that affect a small number of panel participants. There is no way for the researcher to know which panel members will be so affected. The researcher can anticipate the extent of attrition due to mortality by calculating the expected number of deaths for the panel from demographic life tables.

Failure to locate respondents may occur due to such circumstances as changes in telephone numbers or street names by public utilities. Respondents may change residence without leaving forwarding addresses. Or respondents may try to keep their whereabouts unknown to avoid disruption of their private lives or prosecution for unlawful acts. The failure to contact a respondent may also occur because of the behaviors of gatekeepers—people who are not in the panel themselves but who control access to panel members. For example, parents may refuse to report the whereabouts of a son or daughter. Gatekeepers increase the probability that contact may not be made with certain panel members.

Whatever the reason for the loss of contact with the respondent, failure to locate is potentially the most likely source of attrition. About thirty years ago, researchers were advised to expect a loss of 25 percent or more of panel members in national studies (Campbell and Katona 1953). In recent years, however, tracking methodologies have progressed to the point where almost all respondents are located if the researcher develops a sound track-ing design, allocates sufficient resources, and uses effective tracking pro-cedures.

Inability to interview a respondent occurs because the researcher fails to allow sufficient time or provide convenient scheduling for the interview process. Call-backs and multiple mailings take time but are successful tech-niques for contacting respondents who are not at home or are busy at the time of the initial contact. The hours during which interviewing takes place and the season of the year affect the number of call-backs required.

The largest source of attrition after locating a sample is refusal to par-ticipate. In cross-sectional studies, refusals and questionnaire nonresponse are a major concern. Refusals have been reported at over 80 percent (Kanuk and Berenson 1975). Nonresponse to sensitive questions occurs frequently. Although earlier cooperation in the study may minimize the amount of nonresponse in panel designs, respondent refusals are a problem in all panel studies.

Finally, information mismanagement as a source of attrition includes loss of address information, interview records, and questionnaires. These are clearly researcher errors.

Of the six major sources of attrition, failure to locate respondents and refusal to participate present the most serious methodological problems. Because panel members cannot be replaced and data are needed for all measurement points in order to have a valid case in panel analyses, the researcher must locate the panel member and do so in a way that encourages that person to continue participation in the study. High panel attrition may produce sample bias, especially if those who are not restudied have attitudes or behaviors that differ from those who participate. Although there are statistical methods available to weight data to adjust for nonresponse bias, application of these methods is complex and requires assumptions about the nature of nonresponse (Alwin 1977). A better strategy places emphasis on reducing attrition, thereby precluding most nonrandom sample bias.[3] The Comprehensive Tracking Model provides a logic for why people respond to requests for information and a set of principles and considerations to ensure that most, if not all, of the panel members are contacted.

Organization of the Book

This book contains seven chapters. Chapter 2, which develops the Com-prehensive Tracking Model, provides a theoretical rationale for why people participate in panel studies and informs the design of tracking strategies that reduce panel attrition. Chapter 3 presents a review of previous ex-perience with three major tracking approaches. The advantages and disadvantages of each approach are weighed together with a summary statement of the best ways to implement the methods. Chapter 4 details sources of information that can be used to track panel members. We introduce a strategy for sequencing the sources to increase tracking efficiency. Chapter 5 reviews the development of a tracking strategy for the Career Development Study. The Comprehensive Tracking Model is applied to guide decisions concerning the type, mode of implementation, and sequencing of methods used in the study. Chapter 6 reports the results achieved through the tracking strategy. We evaluate the design, present characteristics of the people who were easy or difficult to locate, and report detailed costs for mail and telephone techniques. The book concludes with a discussion of areas that require further research, federal regulations and ethical issues, and reflections on the importance of tracking for research and society.

Notes

1. The literature reflects considerable diversity in use of the terms *longitudinal*, *panel*, and *follow-up* research. In part, the varied use originates because longitudinal methods developed across disciplines, notably sociology, psychology, anthropology, economics, medicine, and education. In an effort to structure this literature, we propose the following typology and observe these definitions.

Longitudinal designs refer to a genre of designs that require observations at more than one point in time. There are three major types of longitudinal designs: the classic experiment, the trend, and the panel. The designs differ in the extent of control exercised by the researcher and in subject characteristics. In the *classic experiment design*, the same subjects or groups are observed at two or more points in time and the researcher has extensive control over the events that occur between observations. The *trend study* is a longitudinal design in which the researcher has little control over the events that transpire, except for the timing of the observations. The observations are made on different samples of subjects from the same population. A *cohort study* is a special case of a trend study in which the researcher makes observations on different samples of subjects from a population that shares similar experiences—for example, a birth cohort. A *panel study* is a design that requires information from the same subjects at two or more points in time and, aside from timing the observations, the researcher has little control over the events that occur between observations. A *follow-up study* is a special type of panel design in which initial data were obtained from sources other than the subjects of the study (for example, school or medical records) and the subjects remain in contact with the researcher or are tracked by the researcher for a second observation.

2. See Kish (1965) for additional details on these sources of non-response.

3. Response errors also introduce bias. See Alwin (1977) for a discussion of various forms of survey error.

2 The Comprehensive Tracking Model

The Comprehensive Tracking Model is a logic that informs why people participate in surveys and a set of procedures for the researcher to use in implementing that logic in panel studies. The model, simple yet inclusive, can be applied in a variety of panel study situations. Application of the model to the Career Development Study demonstrates its power and success.

In this chapter we present the Comprehensive Tracking Model in four parts. First, we present a rationale for why people respond to surveys. This logic guides the overall design and the day-to-day implementation of the tracking strategy. Second, we identify the parameters of the tracking strategy. The parameter values vary from one study to another. The challenge is to assess them accurately in a particular circumstance and to integrate them into an effective tracking effort. Third, we present a set of organizational principles that govern implementation of the model. Fourth, we consider shortcomings of earlier tracking efforts, outline how the Comprehensive Tracking Model addresses those concerns, make the case for developing a comprehensive tracking strategy, and urge that the design be evaluated in a rigorous pilot test prior to use. The model is heuristic. It is both a working model for varied application and an evolving framework that is a basis for further refinement.

The goal of the Comprehensive Tracking Model is to maximize sample relocation and response rates and to do so efficiently and economically. The model minimizes attrition caused by respondents who refuse to participate and respondent cases that are lost. Lost cases occur when respondents are not found and when respondents are found but move to new residences that are not located.

The relocation of respondents in panel studies is part of the larger research effort designed to elicit valid and reliable information from study participants. Because tracking is not an end in itself but a means to an end, the goal of the larger effort—to gather valid and reliable information from respondents—must inform the design and execution of the tracking strategy. Simple head counts are not enough. Indeed, tracking success becomes tracking failure if the relocation effort jeopardizes the data-gathering response rate or the quality of the data. The success of a tracking effort, then, can be determined only when the quality of the data is established.

The task is to reestablish contact with panel members. At a minimum, renewed contact must leave the respondent at ease and attitudinally neutral about the prospect of further participation in the study. Renewed contact must ensure that the desired relationship with the respondent is not jeopardized.

Why People Respond

Successful tracking fundamentally means eliciting cooperative behavior from respondents. At the core of the Comprehensive Tracking Model is a logic to explain why people respond. The rationale is informed by concepts drawn from the literature on social psychology. We examine three sets of issues.

First, tracking involves respondent behavior. We ask: What causes that behavior? The source of the respondent's behavior most accessible to the researcher's influence is the respondent's attitudes. The central question is this: What are attitudes and how can the appropriate attitudes be formed in the respondent? Tracking involves attitudes, attitude formation, and attitude change.

Second, generating the appropriate respondent attitudes is not sufficient. When or under what conditions do attitudes cause behavior that is consistent with the attitudes? Tracking involves the attitude-behavior relationship.

Third, tracking involves not just any behavior but a special type of respondent behavior. One form of respondent behavior is refusal to participate. Another is cooperation. What causes helping behavior? Tracking involves prosocial or helping behavior.

These are the central issues, each reduced to a key question. The answers to the questions are the basis of the Comprehensive Tracking Model and provide the rationale for why people participate in panel studies.

Attitudes and Attitude Formation

Attitudes are enduring, generalized, learned predispositions (Zimbardo and Ebbesen 1969; Zimbardo, Ebbesen, and Maslach 1977). They are composed of cognitive, affective, and behavioral components. They include likes and dislikes, affinities for and aversions to people, groups, situations, objects, research projects, and other identifiable aspects in the environment.

In the case of tracking, respondents typically do not have well-formed attitudes about the content of the study, the goals of the research, or the procedures that are followed. The researcher's challenge is to create new attitudes for the respondent. The task is pedagogical, a matter of providing information.

Two respondent attitudes are particularly important and are linked to helping behavior in survey research. The first is that the researchers are credible and legitimate, and what they are doing is worthwhile. The second is that the respondent's participation is important. The research is useful. It might even be helpful to the respondent, if only indirectly. Moreover, participation will not harm or be unduly burdensome to the respondent. These are the two central respondent attitudes the researcher needs to cultivate.

How can these attitudes be formed? Zimbardo and Ebbesen (1969) sketched a communications model of attitude formation. The process involves four components that we apply to the tracking effort:

1. Respondent's initial attitude;
2. Attention to the communicator and the message;
3. Comprehension of the information; and
4. Motivation for accepting and responding in terms of the information received.

Typically, potential respondents are unaware of the researcher's plans and therefore are neutral about participation. Anecdotal evidence supports this assumption. Usually nearly half of potential respondents will reply to an unannounced, single effort to gather information. The initial challenge, then, is to get the potential respondent's attention.

Before the respondent can process and act on information, the message must be received. The researcher has the dual tasks of getting and holding the attention of his or her subject. The initial signal and message must be geared to the audience; it must be neither so simple that it is dismissed nor so complex that it is ignored. The researcher must calculate the amount of information for every step in the tracking and data-gathering effort because the message, whether simple or complex, must be understood by the respondent.

The Comprehensive Tracking Model is informed by a communications model of attitude formation. The communications model identifies the several features of the anticipated researcher-respondent interaction that can be varied by the researcher. There are four elements: information about the researcher, information about the message, information about the respondents, and information about behavioral expectations and norms. The researcher creates appropriate attitudes in respondents by adjusting the information content, timing the information flow, and calibrating the amount of information as it relates to the researcher, the message, the respondent, and the expected behavior.

The Attitude-Behavior Relationship

Given that appropriate respondent attitudes are formed, under what conditions do attitudes cause behaviors? Several propositions from research on the attitude-behavior relationship inform this query (Schuman and Johnson 1976; Schwartz 1977, 1978; Heberlein and Black 1976):

1. Attitudes are most effective for influencing behavior when the attitudes are specific to the desired behavior and involve behavioral intention. For example, an attitude favorable to youth is more desirable if the study is about youth than is a humanitarian attitude toward people in general.
2. Attitudes are more likely to result in corresponding behavior when the desired attitudes are salient to the potential respondent. For example, an attitude favorable to youth is more likely to produce the desired behavior if the respondent has a vested interest in youth or has recently thought about or dealt with youth.
3. Attitudes are more likely to cause behavior that is consistent with the attitude when the attitude is formed or made salient in temporal proximity to the desired behavior. For example, creating a favorable attitude toward youth is more likely to produce the desired behavior if the attitude is generated or made salient shortly before the behavior is requested.
4. Contradictory situational pressures to behave inconsistent with the attitude should be minimized. For example, contacts should be avoided during normal meal preparation and eating hours. Contacting the respondent at work may interfere with job duties or violate company policy.

These attitude-behavior relationships undergird the logic in the Comprehensive Tracking Model for how and when respondents are contacted.

Helping Behavior

Even with the appropriate attitudes and optimal attitude-behavior congruence, the cooperative behavior required in successful tracking occurs in a a larger framework of situations, interactions, persons, and personalities. What causes helping behavior in these contexts? The research on helping or prosocial behavior is conveniently summarized in a conceptual distinction provided by Piliavin and colleagues (Piliavin, Rodin, and Piliavin 1969; Piliavin and Piliavin 1972; see also Schwartz 1977).

Piliavin and others reason that in social contexts where a person is confronted with an emergency situation, the individual encounters competing costs. On the one hand, the request is costly to the individual because, at a minimum, meeting the request requires some time and effort. On the other hand, saying "no" or ignoring the request also exacts costs, in the form, perhaps, of guilt feelings or a tarnished reputation. The point is that the person who is asked to help will confront costs for both helping and not helping. The question is this: What costs are the potential respondent most likely to accept?

The Piliavin paradigm differs in three important respects from the respondent situation in a panel study. First, Piliavin and Piliavin study emergency situations. Whether respondents participate in the second wave of a panel study cannot fairly be characterized as a comparable dire circumstance. Second, Piliavin and Piliavin seek to explain bystander or third-party intervention. We apply the logic to more direct second-party involvement. Third, in the Piliavin studies the bystander is not confronted with a direct request for help. That is the situation in our research paradigm.

There are nontrivial differences, then, in the intent of the Piliavin paradigm and our application of the prosocial model. Nonetheless, the paradigm is instructive for anticipating responses to simple requests for help. Where physical and emotional arousal is a condition for helping in an emergency situation, getting the attention of the potential helper is the precondition for helping in the tracking situation. Unless a researcher gets and holds the respondent's attention, communication of information is minimal, and the respondent is more likely to behave as if dealing with a stranger.

Once the attention of the respondent is obtained, however, the researcher can present information that establishes a new respondent attitude favorable to cooperation. Such an attitude suggests that the researcher deserves help, that help is needed, and that the respondent can provide the needed help. As attitudes are created or changed in favor of cooperation and response, it becomes costly for the respondent to ignore the request and refuse to help.

The request for help also involves costs for helping. Disruption of schedule, time lost, effort expended, and the disapproval of others are but a few of the costs for helping a researcher. Some of the costs for helping can be minimized by the researcher through careful planning and timing of contacts. For example, telephoning a respondent at work can be avoided. But some costs cannot be anticipated—for example, disrupting a diaper change or a shower. How the researcher deals with the anticipated and unanticipated demands placed on the respondent will determine the respondent's level of costs for helping.

In short, given the attention of the respondent, favorable attitudes, and attitude-behavior congruence, cooperation from the respondent will be a function of costs for helping and costs for not helping. We submit these predictions that govern participation in panel studies:

1. If attitudes favorable to helping are elicited and the costs for helping are minimized, the likelihood of obtaining the desired information increases.

2. If the costs of helping are high and the attitude of the respondent is not favorable, the likelihood that the respondent will refuse to help increases.

3. If attitudes are favorable to helping but the cost of helping is also high, the respondent will likely refuse to give a direct response but refer the request to someone else or provide a partial response or just enough help to assuage guilt.[1]

4. Finally, if attitudes are not favorable toward responding or the cost of not helping is low and the cost of helping is also low, the respondent's response cannot be predicted. The respondent's behavior is due to other factors. Perhaps the respondent had nothing else to do and therefore responds. This is an apathy situation, and the respondent may discard a questionnaire, dismiss the request, or terminate the interaction at the slightest provocation.

We submit that people have reasons for behaving as they do and that the challenge in motivating favorable responses is to give potential respondents reasons for enacting the desired behavior. Our reply to why people respond in panel studies is based on an understanding of the attitude-behavior and helping-behavior literatures. To maximize the likelihood of a response, steps should be taken to get the respondent's attention, to develop an attitude favorable to providing a response, to minimize the costs a respondent must bear in providing help, and to make salient the personal and social costs for not helping.

Parameters Governing Tracking Strategies

The key to successful tracking is a strategy that provides for contact with each panel member in a way that maximizes response. In this section we identify the study parameters that the researcher must consider in formulating a tracking strategy tailored to the research requirements.

A tracking strategy is a detailed plan for establishing contact with panel members. It is based on a logic that informs why people participate in panel studies. The same logic applies to the day-to-day decisions involved in implementing the strategy. Tracking strategies vary in the type, number, extensiveness, and sequencing of techniques that are used. Although an optimal plan applicable to all research situations does not exist, we identify four general parameters that govern the combination of elements that best serve a study's purposes. The parameters are resources, time, panel characteristics, and respondent characteristics.

We emphasize the importance of doing an advanced systematic analysis of the proposed tracking requirements and of making an equally thorough inventory of available resources. The Comprehensive Tracking Model requires an optimal fit among the underlying logic for the tracking strategy, the study-specific requirements, and the resources available to the researcher. The underlying logic sensitizes the researcher to critical issues in the study requirements. It also prompts the researcher to be expansive and creative in figuring out ways to meet the study requirements.

Figure 2-1 illustrates how resources, time, panel characteristics, and respondent characteristics enter the assessment of anticipated tracking difficulties, the particular study requirements, and the available resources.

Resources

The available resources typically consist of budgets, physical facilities, supplies, services, and personnel. Institutions usually provide office space, equipment, supplies, and services as part of an employment package or make these available at favorable rates. In most instances, printing facilities, mass-mailing equipment, computers, telephone services, vehicles, and the like are also available.

The departmentalization of institutions may obscure the availability of particular services or facilities, and it may be worth the effort to inquire about the services, equipment, and expertise that are available in large organizations. The business department, the registrar's office, or the alumni office in a college or university may have access to mass-mailing equipment. The assessment of resources should be extended to include services provided by outside vendors. For example, if there is limited capacity to generate a mass mailing inside the institution, it may be cost efficient to contract with an outside vendor for the service.

The researcher may not be familiar with recent developments in communications technology. For that matter, the investigator may not know what resources are locally available. The researcher may want to meet with a local office-equipment dealer regarding which firms have purchased word-processing stations or document printers. The dealer may refer to a secretarial service, bank, school district, real estate office, or insurance company that provides the services needed.

Finding experienced trackers and supervisory personnel may be difficult. The required skills are unique and technical. If qualified personnel are not available, resources will be needed to train recruits to do the tracking or to purchase the services from an established organization. Personnel, together with budgets, equipment, supplies, and services, are the general resource base for tracking. In combination these resources are the major determinants of the number, type, and extensiveness of tracking approaches that can be employed.

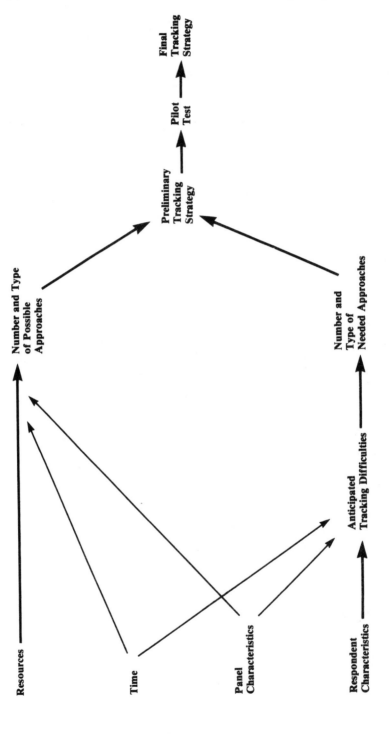

Figure 2-1. Elements of Tracking Strategy Development in the Comprehensive Tracking Model

Time

Time bears on tracking difficulties in two ways. First, as the amount of time between panel observations increases, tracking becomes more difficult. A long-term design increases the likelihood that respondents have moved or died and the likelihood that the respondents' references have also moved or died.

But there are ways to overcome these deficits. Suppose, for example, that the researcher is restudying former high school students, as is often the case. Where the research design allows, the problems associated with the time elapsed between observations may be reduced by planning the tracking effort to follow shortly after high school class reunions. The community searches made by reunion committees are sometimes very thorough. Class-reunion committees have access to social networks and information sources that are not available to the researcher. If the researcher can enlist the cooperation of the reunion committee, much of the work may already be accomplished.

Second, the time scheduled for completion of the tracking effort affects what tracking approaches are possible. In most instances, time makes demands on resources. If only a short time is scheduled for tracking, multiple mailings may not be possible, and more costly tracking approaches may be required. Moreover, if insufficient time is scheduled for tracking, the problem of locating hard-to-find respondents is substantially increased. Work patterns and seasonal work cycles for traveling salespeople, commercial fishing people, loggers, and construction workers require that adequate time be allowed to locate the hard-to-find. Making generous time allowances entails costs, however. As the time required for tracking increases, the costs for personnel, equipment, and facilities also increase.

We urge that tracking be completed within one year of initiation. This pragmatic upper limit accommodates postal regulations that mandate that mail be forwarded only for a period of one year. It avoids stretching tracking across two summers during which respondent mobility increases. It keeps tracking and data collection within a reasonable and manageable time frame. Finally, it minimizes change over time in variables that are important to the researcher. The minimal amount of time that should be scheduled will be determined largely by the sequencing of approaches.

Under optimal tracking conditions, a sequence of three or four mailings requires about ten weeks to locate 50 to 55 percent of the panel members. The time required for telephone tracking is somewhat less. Suppose, for example, that to locate five thousand panel members who left high school ten years ago in a particular state requires an average of twenty minutes of personnel time per respondent. Then ten interviewers working evenings and weekends (each working twenty-six hours per week) would require about

6.4 weeks to track 85 to 90 percent of this panel of young adults. Community visits take considerably longer than either mail or telephone approaches. Under ideal conditions, a well-organized effort might locate about 90 percent of five thousand panel members in as little as two months. However, four to six months is a more reasonable lower limit if multiple approaches are used and if time is allowed for local community information sources to seek out information on the hard-to-find.

Panel Characteristics

Panel size refers to the number of respondents included in the panel. *Panel dispersion* is the geographic distribution of panel members and establishes the geographic scope of the tracking effort. If telephone or personal visit approaches are used, the time required for tracking will relate directly to panel size and dispersion. Panel size and dispersion do not necessarily affect the timetable for a mail approach, but they do increase the need for high-speed equipment and related personnel costs.

Aside from the costs involved in processing more cases, panel size and dispersion affect resources in other ways. For example, increased panel size and dispersion require more efficient record-keeping procedures. If a panel is drawn from a city that has low out-migration, a larger panel size increases time spent making community visits, but the sequence of visits can be planned and made more efficient. As the panel increases in size and becomes more dispersed, community visits become less cost-effective. Mail and telephone approaches are not necessarily less efficient with increased size and dispersion.

At what point does panel size make a difference? It is useful to consider the implication of size for arbitrary groupings. Small studies of, say, one hundred respondents who live in reasonable proximity can usually be accomplished by any combination of tracking approaches that is convenient. With small panels, economies of scale do not apply, and the tasks of record keeping and material preparation can be managed without special equipment.

Increasing the panel size to several thousand means increased numbers of respondents and more dispersion. Record keeping for medium-sized studies requires some form of automation. Telephone and mail approaches become more cost and time efficient than personal visits. Access to automated equipment becomes a necessity.

Large panel studies of more than four thousand respondents present extraordinary problems. Automation and mass production of mail materials are imperative. For practical and financial considerations, the approach options in very large panels reduce to making contact with most panel members with mass mailings and then turning to other tracking approaches that are more individualized but incur higher personnel costs.

Another characteristic of panels that contributes to tracking difficulty and cost is the amount of identifying information on panel members in the data base. Usually researchers do not gather information from respondents that will assist later tracking efforts. The information that is useful includes the following:

1. Full name of the panel member; middle initials or names are frequently necessary.
2. Previous mailing addresses.
3. Birth date and birthplace.
4. Father's and mother's full name and address; mother's maiden name is sometimes useful.
5. Names and addresses of two or three close relatives or guardians.
6. Names and addresses of best friends.
7. Driver's license number.
8. Social security number.
9. Military identification number.
10. Name and address of current or former employer.
11. Names and addresses of parents' employers.

In most cases surprisingly little information is required to locate a person. The respondent's full name and previous address may be sufficient. However, it is not possible to anticipate who will be difficult to locate at a future date and what information will assist that effort. Obtaining more information earlier makes it less difficult to track respondents later.

Respondent Characteristics

Resources, time, and panel characteristics constrain the number and type of tracking approaches that can be used. Time and panel characteristics also determine the difficulty of tracking. As illustrated in figure 2-1, respondent characteristics determine tracking difficulty and the number and type of approaches that are needed.[2] Several respondent characteristics are known to affect ease of tracking.

Urban or rural residence affects tracking requirements (Crider and Willits 1973; Clarridge, Sheehy, and Hauser 1977; Barnes 1972). Rural respondents are relatively easy to find through social networks, and the availability of rural social networks tends to compensate for the general lack of detail in rural addresses. Although working through social networks is usually not as effective in urban areas, neighbors and friends often provide useful leads for locating mobile families. A lack of extensive social networks in urban areas can usually be overcome by intensive searches of old telephone directories and city directories that identify past neighbors who may know the person's current whereabouts. Also, families living in cities usually have more accurate numerical addresses than do families with rural route numbers or post-office boxes.

Lack of accurate addresses does not mean that the post office cannot or will not deliver mail in small communities. In large cities a change of residence, even if only a few blocks away, is likely to result in undeliverable mail if a change-of-address form is not filed at the post office. But under current postal operations, letters mailed to families in rural areas are usually forwarded to the correct individuals. While recent efforts to close rural postal stations could dramatically affect these forwarding practices, the extensive social networks in rural communities and the personal knowledge of the local carrier undoubtedly account for successes in forwarding mail in rural America.

The literature documents the difficulties of tracking minorities. Nonwhites are harder to track than whites (Bright 1967), although the reasons are not clear. Minorities, especially foreign born, are more likely to have had name changes (Wilcox 1965) and to have unlisted telephone numbers (Glasser and Metzger 1975). This undoubtedly contributes to the problem. Moreover, lack of researcher knowledge of minority life-styles and minority suspicions regarding the researcher's motives for making contact suggest that minority interviewers be used (Lewis 1972). While there is no evidence that the major tracking approaches do not work for minorities, the problems of name changes and unlisted telephone numbers may make mail and telephone approaches less efficient than community visits in the case of minorities.

Several other respondent characteristics bear on tracking success. Families may withhold information about family members who are in prison or in trouble with the law (Homans 1972). Also family problems that lead to divorce or separation typically result in family members' reluctance to provide information (Bright 1967). Another problem is that social networks are disrupted in neighborhoods undergoing rapid change, and informal information sources may be lacking (Willits, Crider, and Bealer 1969).

Generally it is more difficult to contact families of lower socioeconomic status (Bright 1967; Coombs and Freedman 1964). Such families are less likely to own residences and maintain stable employment patterns that provide leads in tracking.

People who do not participate in formal organizations are more difficult to locate (Crider and Willits 1973). Their names do not appear on membership lists, which rules out that information source.

Older people are easier to locate than younger people (Bright 1967). Age may be a factor because more younger people have unlisted telephone numbers than do older people (Glasser and Metzger 1975). The young are also more mobile (U.S. Department of Commerce 1980a).

Gender differences have not been reported (Bright 1967; Willits, Crider, and Bealer 1969), but more single women have unlisted telephone numbers, and women may have name changes that likely increase tracking difficulties.

It is more difficult to locate military personnel because of their high mobility and lack of social integration in stable communities.

Finally, childless couples are more likely to move (Coombs and Freedman 1964). Families with several children are less likely to move. When moves occur, families with several children are more likely to move out of the community.

Each of these poses difficulties that require adjustments in the tracking strategy. Typically this means using multiple approaches.

In summary, the available resources, the time frame for completing the tracking, the time elapsed between first and subsequent observations, panel characteristics, and respondent characteristics are parameters that must be taken into account in formulating a tracking design. Careful advanced assessment of the parameters must be made, and resources must be tailored to the study requirements. The assessment of parameters and anticipated tracking difficulties provides a sense of what is ideally needed, on the one hand, and what is realistically possible, on the other. The researcher achieves an ideal tracking design to the extent that the number and type of needed approaches can be provided.

Tracking Principles

Three principles govern organizing the tracking effort and implementing the tracking design. They are drawn from our reading of the literature and our own experience. The principles are complemented by related observations that further inform execution of the tracking design.

Organization of the Tracking Effort

The organization principles can be briefly stated: simplicity, diversity, and automation. Diversity and simplicity may appear to be incongruous; nonetheless, each is relevant to successful tracking.

Simplicity. The principle of simplicity suggests that the researcher reduce tracking tasks to the most elementary level of complexity and organization possible. Simplicity focuses the tracking effort on locating respondents. It requires removing all tasks and organizational preoccupations that detract from the tracking effort.

If personnel are expected to locate study participants and collect data concurrently, the tracking effort may be relegated to second place and fragmented. Dual assignments invariably reduce the perceived importance of tracking and may create confusion among trackers.

Multiple tracking centers also tend to introduce organizational hierarchies and distance between the principal investigators and the trackers. The result can be loss of control and increased difficulty in communication.

Whenever possible, therefore, the tracking effort should be the sole activity of a trained group operating out of a central facility. A person who understands the objectives of the study and the logic of the tracking design should supervise the effort.

Diversity. The more tracking approaches that are applied, the greater is the probability of locating all panel members. Current addresses can be found for all but a small number of people in our society. Very few—perhaps 2 to 4 percent of the general population—try not to be found or are extremely mobile and never have a permanent address. Finding the other 96 to 98 percent depends on using approaches that implement the logic for why people participate in panel studies.

Finding panel members may require various approaches, and it makes sense to calibrate the approach to the difficulty of the task. Envision a multiple-approach strategy that is analogous to a series of sifting screens (Wilcox 1965). A coarse, inexpensive screen is used first to catch large numbers of potential respondents, but at some point the large screen fails, and smaller objects fall through. A more refined and, perhaps, somewhat more expensive screen catches those who fell through the coarse screen. More refined screens are introduced until only a few objects pass through the most expensive and extremely fine screens.

An efficient tracking design uses multiple, sequenced screens such that each more refined and expensive screen captures the most respondents at the least cost. For some people one approach will work; for others it will fail. Tracking success occurs when backup plans economically catch the failures of earlier approaches. Diversity in approaches increases the probability that one of the screens will catch every respondent. The researcher's planning and knowledge increase the probability that the design will catch most respondents in the early, most efficient, and economical screens.

Automation. Tracking is an information-processing task. Based on available information, a tracker looks for new information that will assist the search. The tracker records the results of every effort because earlier information may be useful in later efforts to contact the hard-to-locate. In large panel studies, the tracker's ability to use the information efficiently, to store the results of a tracking effort, and to monitor tracking progress depends on automation almost totally. The third principle of tracking organization is that the researcher automate every possible tracking process.

We sound a note of caution: if automation becomes a limiting factor or an end in itself, then it fails. Automated systems no less than filing systems can become master rather than servant. For example, limiting full names to twenty characters or truncating addresses for ease in computer storage can defeat the purpose of collecting the information and increase the difficulty in tracking. Automated record-systems should serve the requirements of the study, not dictate them.

Tracking Refinements

Once the blueprint for the tracking effort is drafted, attention shifts to refining the various tracking approaches. The refinements are intangibles that can give tracking an artistic flavor, a touch of class that distinguishes the total effort. The refinements introduce a sense of professionalism to what is done and how it is done. Together with the underlying logic for why people participate in follow-up studies, the refinements integrate the tracking approaches into a coherent strategy and process. Three refinements to the approaches are clarity, competence, and persistence.

Clarity. Clarity is the implementation analog to organizational simplicity. Clarity must be the hallmark of all communications with respondents. A straightforward and uncomplicated statement increases the likelihood that a message will be comprehended. Comprehension is the first step toward the desired behavioral response. Succinctness in presenting the who, what, where, when, how, and why of the study to panel members conveys the critical information the researcher wants participants to receive. Raising superfluous issues risks confusing participants. Moreover, it frustrates respondent efforts to identify what is wanted, to process information, and to conclude that help should be provided. Clarity also applies to making the request for help explicit so that behavioral expectations are defined and unambiguous.

Competence. Competence refers to the image the researcher projects by the manner in which the tracking effort is carried out. Attention to detail, precision, and flawlessness in interactions with respondents legitimates the information conveyed. If the researcher states that the study is important, that it will make a valuable contribution to society, that it is conducted in a scientific manner by a legitimate institution, the researcher's presentation of self and the project should not conflict with that message. Misspelled words, poor quality printing, amateur procedures, and failure to follow through with promises may convey impressions of incompetence and raise doubts about the legitimacy or importance of the message.

The mark of competence affects the tracking effort in yet another way. The manner in which project staff conduct the tracking conveys the project image most directly and, therefore, is a major determinant of success rates. Attention to detail, recording information correctly, observing the suggested protocols in dealing with respondents, courtesy, and anticipating the concerns of respondents are skills that should be cultivated by project staff. These elements of style either support or conflict with the formal message the researcher conveys.

Persistence. Persistence is also important to tracking success. Barnes (1972) expressed the need for personnel who "have St. Bernard instincts as well as Bulldog tenacity." The necessary attitudes and traits that characterize successful trackers are a compulsiveness to check every piece of information and a sense of adventure in following reasonable leads to their conclusion. Sometimes persistence is nothing more than tenacity in searching for information and leads. At other times persistence is knowing when to be patient, or to wait, or to encourage an information source to help locate a critical lead. A tracking strategy that does not encourage persistence pays a cost in relocation rates.

Developing a Tracking Strategy

One shortcoming of less-than-successful tracking efforts is that the logic for what prompts people to participate focused on "bags of tricks" rather than on principles of human behavior. A second reason for less-than-satisfactory outcomes is that the parameters of the tracking effort—resources, time, panel characteristics, and respondent characteristics—were not carefully considered in advance and integrated with a logic of human behavior. A third area of tracking failure involves project organization. Personnel were required to attend to various and, perhaps, conflicting tasks. Fourth, the financial and efficiency advantages of automation were not fully explored. In some instances, total reliance was placed on a single approach, and plans were not made to compensate for tracking failure. Finally, integrating the logic, parameters, and project organization into a coherent design was left to chance rather than objective planning.

The components of the Comprehensive Tracking Model provide the researcher with a plan for overcoming these shortcomings. The first component of the model focuses on why people respond to requests for help. The second focuses on the parameters that must be integrated into a tracking strategy. The third component outlines principles of organizing the tracking effort. Each component describes an important element that should be considered in developing a tracking strategy.

An understanding of why people respond provides the basis for the entire tracking effort. The rationale ensures the continued cooperation of panel members and maintains data quality. Tracking parameters provide the guideposts for decisions about what kind of tracking strategies are needed and what strategies are possible within available resources. The principles of tracking organization are the precepts that govern tracking. The principles promote a tracking strategy that is organized efficiently and includes sufficient diversity in approach to ensure that all or most panel members are contacted.

Developing a tracking strategy is a process of judiciously choosing the proper mixture of tracking approaches that will maximize respondent contacts. The strategy includes a detailed plan for implementing the approaches that is consistent with the tracking rationale and organizational principles.

An important component of advanced preparation is determining how well the design works, where its soft spots are, and what the outcome of the tracking strategy is likely to be. This information can be obtained from a pilot study of selected respondents. The adjustments suggested by a pilot study fine-tune the tracking strategy and make the main tracking task that of monitoring compliance with the plan rather than belatedly fixing up ill-conceived tracking notions that fail. The Comprehensive Tracking Model provides the guidelines that make tracking more than an art or craft.

The issues that confront researchers undertaking tracking efforts include deciding what tracking approaches should be included in the strategy; in what order they should appear; what approaches should be used extensively; and what approaches should be held in reserve.

Notes

1. An indirect response typically occurs when a relative is asked for a family member's current address. This is particularly true when there are problems in family relationships. Usually the relative will provide only the parent's address.

2. Respondent characteristics do not affect the number or type of approaches that are possible. While a panel study of deaf children would dramatically affect the type of approaches needed, the characteristics do not affect what a researcher can do. If a researcher does not have the facilities to produce letters, however, an assessment of the approaches needed and what is possible would indicate that the researcher is not prepared to track deaf respondents successfully.

3 Tracking Approaches

There are three major approaches to tracking panel members: mail, telephone calls, and community visits. The goal is to find the respondent as effectively and efficiently as possible. Effectiveness is measured by location rates and data quality. Efficiency is measured by dollars spent. The optimal strategy meets the success goals within the available resources. A researcher improves the probabilities of success by considering the advantages and disadvantages of the major tracking approaches and by understanding the relationship between tracking parameters and different tracking approaches.

The Mail Approach

The mail approach is the most economical for contacting people who do not move frequently or do not have a telephone or are not trying to conceal their whereabouts. The economy accrues from the services provided by the post office and the extent to which the researcher can automate mailing tasks. Unlike the telephone and community-visit approaches, the mail approach pays others to locate and deliver a message. This reduces personnel costs and takes advantage of established postal services to track people.

Although the cost per letter for mass printing and bulk mailing is nominal, the cost per address obtained can be high if the researcher does not recognize the limitations of the mail approach. Postal regulations and standardized communications are two major limitations of the mail approach. The mail approach is the least flexible of the approaches and the most impersonal.

The Postal Service

The postal service functions as a giant tracking organization for the minor cost of postage. If mail is to be delivered or forwarded, however, the researcher must adhere to regulations governing postal services.

The post office offers two classes of mail delivery and services that are useful for tracking: first- and third-class mail. Personal correspondence must be sent by first-class mail. A letter sent by first-class mail is delivered to the address, forwarded to a new address, or returned to the sender marked why the letter was not delivered. The post office forwards first-class mail to a new address for a period of one year following the change of address.

Third-class mail consists of printed notices and brochures. It must not contain personal correspondence. Third-class mail is less expensive than first-class mail because it provides only the delivery component of the postal service. The post office discards third-class mail if delivery cannot be made to the addressee.[1]

The post office provides other services that assist tracking. When the researcher indicates "address correction requested" on the envelope, the new address to which a letter was forwarded will be provided to the sender.[2] This service is cost efficient because only mail that is actually forwarded results in a charge to the sender.

Certified mail is expensive but provides a record that the letter was delivered. Certified mail heightens the importance of the correspondence because it requires a signature on receipt. If the respondent is not home, the postal service leaves a nondelivery notice, and the recipient must go to the post office to sign for the letter. A boomerang effect may occur if the recipient must travel some distance to get the "important letter" and finds that it merely requests help in updating an address (Slocum, Empey, and Swanson 1956). In most tracking situations, however, this risk may be necessary in order to establish exactly to whom and where a letter is delivered.

Business Reply Mail can reduce the expense of return postage if it is likely that a large percentage of people will not respond to a request. The saving depends on the arrangements that are made with the post office.[3] While business reply provides some savings, the researcher must weigh other costs. Consideration must be given to the image communicated to the respondent by having "Business Reply Mail" visible on the return envelope. Appeals to the scientific and humanitarian nature of the study may appear to be inconsistent with a return envelope that prominently displays the word *business*.

Communication by Mail

The image portrayed by a letter signals the major limitation of the mail approach. Mass communication, in whatever the form, is usually not as effective in eliciting attitude change and helping behavior as a personal message to individuals. The mail approach is a one-way communication. It does not enlist dialogue or readily tailor the message to the situation.

In addition, the researcher lacks control over who receives the communication and when it is opened. One spouse may regularly sort their spouse's mail and discard "junk" mail. To successfully counter gatekeeper effects, the researcher must write the letter to create a positive attitude. The letter must be persuasive in appearance and content to people other than the respondent. In the mail situation, the researcher's ability to communicate the importance of the message depends on the sophistication of the available equipment.

Mass-mailing technology has progressed remarkably in recent years. The impersonal "Dear Occupant," "Dear Resident," or "Dear Participant" are no longer serious efforts at tracking people by mail. Neither are computer-printed labels. Equipment exists and is readily available to print the body of the letter and add the address later by computer-assisted processes. The final letter has the appearance of an individually typed letter (see Dillman 1978), not that of a form letter on which names and addresses were obviously typed later. Word-processing equipment, ink-jet document printers, laser printers, and other comparable equipment are even more flexible in that they quickly produce letters adapted to the personal characteristics of the recipient.[4] The quality of the finished letter is very difficult to distinguish from individually typed letters.

These advances are important. Appeals for help in locating people are most successful when they are tailored to the person sought and to the person addressed. State-of-the-art technology provides that flexibility and hard-copy communication power. Although the mail approach cannot compensate for different contexts in which the mail is received and opened, it is possible to present information focused on particular groups and to tap attitudes favorable to a response.

Content of the Tracking Letter. The researcher is usually a stranger to the person contacted. The letter must communicate who is writing the request, what information is requested, why the researcher needs the information, and how and when the recipient should respond. It might appear that lengthy explanations are necessary to inform the reader adequately. However, this is not necessarily the case and, in fact, is not desirable.

Consider, for example, information regarding the sender. It does not require any text. Unlike the telephone approach, visual cues and symbols can identify the sender. A logo or a letterhead specifies the institutional affiliation of the sender. A title under the signature of the sender tells the recipient what role the sender plays in the institution. Thus, the message can be reduced to a few short lines that explain what is requested and when a reply is needed.

Usually the only information required is a full name, a current address, and a telephone number for the person sought. This request can be presented in a single sentence. We suggest that the researcher provide a form for the response that clearly outlines the detail needed for each piece of information.

The researcher can explain why a current address is needed, with a short paragraph highlighting the attitudes the researcher wishes to communicate about the study. There should be sufficient information to permit the potential respondent to decide that the request is important and that a response should be provided. The "keep it simple" formula applies here. Highlighting a large number of peripheral attitudes and raising issues superfluous to the tracking effort will only confuse the potential respondent and lower the probability of a favorable response.

Sending Tracking Letters. The post office delivers millions of pieces of mail each day, much of it bills, notices, surveys, donation requests, promotions, and advertisements. People typically discard or read the content of mail based on a quick assessment of the outer envelope. The impression, not just the information, presented by the envelope determines whether the mail will be opened, read, and answered. The initial impression of the outer envelope must distinguish that letter from other mail if it is to gain the respondent's attention.

How does a researcher convey an impression of importance? Should colored stationery be used, larger than normal envelopes, commemorative stamps, first-class or certified postage, an attractive logo, official stationery, or individually typed addresses? The literature on mail surveys reports contradictory answers (Dillman 1978). The reason for the confusion is the uneven quality of the data, findings based on differing populations, different operationalizations of variables, and radically different response rates reported for studies that examine the effects of techniques on response rates. The conclusions about the effect of techniques on response rates are equivocal.

The techniques associated with Dillman's (1978) Total Design Method are the best example of conflicting reports. The Total Design Method advocates extensive personalization.[5] An alternative position suggests that carefully executed impersonal approaches will be just as successful as the more expensive personalized mailing. Thus, a recent study incorporated a comparison of the Total Design Method and a nonpersonal approach.[6] Both approaches yielded about a 72 percent response. From the perspective of technique, the evidence suggests that a carefully executed study using form letters and labels is as effective and more efficient than the more personalized method. However, viewing the findings from the perspective of why people respond results in a different interpretation.

Information presented to the respondents affects their attitudes about the requests for help. The personalized and nonpersonalized versions of the Pennsylvania study gathered the same information and used the same cover letter but differed in the extensiveness of personalization and the size of envelopes used. Two different impressions about the study were possible.

The nonpersonalized cover letter contained a "Dear Citizen of Pennsylvania" salutation. In addition, "The Citizen's Viewpoint" was printed in large letters on all cover letters and on outgoing and return envelopes.[7] The nonpersonal approach appealed to attitudes held about citizenship, emphasized the importance of the citizen's views, and reminded the respondent about the importance of citizens' informing their elected representatives concerning the future of Pennsylvania. The researchers used group identification effectively to generate attitudes favorable to responding.

The personalized version used Dillman's (1978) procedures to identify the respondent by name on the envelope and cover letter. The outer envelope differentiated the correspondence from junk mail by providing the appearance of a personal letter. The message focused on the person as an individual rather than on the recipient's social role as citizen.

In both the personalized and nonpersonalized versions, the researchers created attitudes favorable to response, and, as a result, the nonpersonalized version was as successful as the personalized in obtaining responses.

We encourage the use of Dillman's (1978) procedures for the mail approach because personalization offers another tool with which the researcher can influence respondent attitudes. We suggest, however, that the researcher give primary attention to forming respondent attitudes that favor response. The manner in which the researcher prepares the outer envelope, the cover letter, the reply form, and the return envelope communicates the only impression the respondent has about the study and tracking effort. The techniques used, whether personalized or nonpersonalized, are inconsequential as long as the message creates attitudes favorable to response. The logic undergirding the Comprehensive Tracking Model emphasizes that the researcher understand the attitudes and characteristics of the panel members and use that knowledge to select the techniques and message that communicate the information the respondent needs in order to make an informed decision to help.

Return Rates

One major concern about the mail approach is the expected response rate using addresses that are five, ten, or fifteen years old. People move and forget or decline to leave forwarding addresses. City officials change street names. Developers raze whole neighborhoods and construct malls. Postal carriers lose or misdeliver mail. The postal service consolidates post offices, changes zip codes, and alters delivery systems. These are but a few of the problems of the mail approach.

Several studies indicate how successful the mail approach is likely to be in tracking people ten or more years after the initial contact. The Adolescent

Society Follow-up Study tracked 9,033 respondents by mail using parents' addresses that were fifteen years old (Temme 1975). The respondents had been enrolled in Illinois high schools during the mid-1950s. The post office delivered about 55 percent of the letters. Half of the parents contacted responded to the first letter and provided a current address for their son or daughter. Temme does not provide the response rates for the second and third mailings to parents but does report that parents eventually supplied 47 percent of all current addresses. This means that about 85 percent of the parents contacted by mail eventually provided a current address for their son or daughter.

The Rural Pennsylvania Panel Study tracked 2,810 sophomores who were enrolled in rural high schools in 1947 (Willits, Crider, and Bealer 1969). The first follow-up was conducted in 1957 and located 83 percent (N = 2,344) of the panel members. The last known addresses were ten years old when the second follow-up letters were mailed in 1967. About 70 percent of the letters were delivered, and 73 percent of the recipients returned a card verifying their current name and address, for 51 percent of the total sample. Almost three-fourths of those who responded replied to the first letter. The remainder responded to a second letter. Willits, Crider, and Bealer (1969) emphasized that the high return by those who received the letter does not reflect respondents' immobility. Over two-thirds of the 1967 addresses confirmed by mail differed from the 1957 address. Most of the responses were received within thirty-five days of the original mailing. Most of the mail that could not be delivered was returned to the investigator within fifteen days of mailing the letters. We will refer to the findings of this study frequently because these researchers located all but 2 of the 2,344 panel members they sought. They also conducted a limited experimental study of the differential effectiveness of tracking procedures.

One of the largest follow-up studies to use a mail approach was Project Talent (Rossi et al. 1976; Wise, McLaughlin, and Steel 1977; Carrel, Potts, and Campbell 1975). A probability sample of all U.S. high-school students in grades 9 through 12 in 1960 (N = 375,122) was followed up one, five, and eleven years after the expected year of graduation from high school. First, the researchers mailed a newsletter. Then they sent a first wave of questionnaires followed by a postcard reminder. They sent a second, third, and fourth mailing of questionnaires to people who did not respond to earlier mailings.[8] Questionnaire mailings included a cover letter and a postage-paid, return envelope. The researchers stamped "address correction requested" on all mailings except those marked *First Class Mail.*

Over the years the project had sent annual newsletters to each participant. A by-product of the newsletters was that the mailings produced forwarding addresses from the post office and the respondent. This procedure resulted in a loss of about 5 percent of the addresses each year (Wise, McLaughlin, and Steel 1977). About a fourth of the original 1960 participants responded to the eleven-year follow-up. The ineffectiveness of the single-method mail-tracking strategy resulted in severe sample attrition and low response rates.

The Telephone Approach

When a potential information provider can be identified and a listed telephone number is available, the telephone tracker can obtain much of the same information that is gained by a community visit. The problems of making the initial telephone contact are offset by numerous advantages: the efficiency with which multiple contacts can be made; the ease of pursuing leads; the opportunity to respond quickly to respondent questions; the administrative advantage of monitoring a centralized tracking organization; and the ability to contact people in areas of high physical risk.

The telephone approach also has several disadvantages. First, if insufficient personal information is available, telephone tracking becomes more difficult because it is not readily apparent who should be contacted. Second, following leads requires considerable personnel time and expensive telephone charges when compared to the time and charges required by the mail approach. Third, trackers may have to collect a modest amount of information before the panel member is located. Fourth, while less restrictive than postal regulations, telephone companies have rules governing the services they provide and the extent of assistance operators will provide. These service restrictions usually mean that only people with listed telephone numbers can be contacted. Fifth, respondents do not have tangible cues to provide information about the legitimacy of the study and request. Even though trackers state that the study is conducted by a reputable organization, a suspicious respondent may still fear deception.

Accurate and detailed record keeping is particularly important in telephone searches in which the tracker has little information. A large number of calls may be made to reconstruct the respondent's social networks. Also, a retrieval system for identifying information is needed so that trackers have ready access to all available information about the panel member. Getting trackers to record neatly all leads pursued in the heat of a search is an ongoing supervisory battle. Finally, it is difficult to find personnel with adequate social skills to cope with respondent questions and detective skills to find the respondents, a problem not encountered in the mail approach.

Telephone-Service Rates and Restrictions

Bell Operating Companies impose few service restrictions that affect tracking, but three are important. First, all Bell companies establish goals and guidelines regarding the number of calls directory-assistance operators are expected to handle over a given period and the amount of time the operators should plan for each directory-assistance call. These goals are used to evaluate operator performance, and operators adjust their time to ensure that performance goals are met. Operators meet their performance goals by restricting the number of listings they will check and by limiting the amount of information they will provide for each number.

Some Bell Operating Companies discourage directory-assistance operators from providing addresses; however, the company realizes the importance of maintaining good customer relations, and this serves the researcher's interests. If a researcher follows procedures that do not make unreasonable demands on operators, operators will respond to requests for assistance.[9]

Second, telephone tracking involves numerous directory-assistance calls. Easily tracked cases average about one call to directory assistance for every long-distance call placed. More difficult cases may require two or three directory-assistance calls. In some areas, a ten- to twenty-cent charge is standard for each directory-assistance call over a limit of five or ten calls per month within the same area code. At the present time, charges are not made for calls to directory assistance outside the caller's area code.

Third, telephone companies charge from 35 to 60 percent less for long-distance calls made in the evening and on weekends. Midday on Saturday and early evenings during the week are optimal contact times for finding people at home (Weeks et al. 1980; Vigderhous 1981), and it may be advisable to schedule telephone tracking to coincide with these optimal times and reduced tariffs.

A researcher will want to explore the availability and relative economies of WATS (Wide Area Telephone Service) lines and other reduced-tariff services for long-distance calls. If these are not available, a researcher contemplating tracking a large number of panel members by telephone must consider the rate structure for various services. Direct-dial rates are not linear functions of distance. It costs about $1.70 to make a five-minute telephone call to Spokane from Seattle, a distance of 278 miles. A similar call from Seattle to New York City, a distance of 2,805 miles, is $2.06—a difference of only $0.36. Currently a person can place any cross-country call during reduced-rate periods and talk for twenty minutes at a cost no greater than $3.84, including tax.

In summary, the researcher should not assume that WATS is less expensive. Our experience with tracking the Career Development Study participants was that prime-time tracking largely coincided with reduced-rate periods. It was more economical for us to use direct-dial services at the reduced rates than to install WATS.

Communication by Telephone

Communicating by telephone poses special problems. Visual cues are not available to legitimize the tracker's request. Unfamiliar speech accents may hinder comprehension and introduce confusion about the legitimacy of the communication. Poor telephone connections and background noise can make the dialogue difficult. Unlike a letter that is attended to at the respondent's convenience, a telephone call interrupts the respondent's normal activities and requires an immediate, albeit minor, behavioral response.

Nonetheless, a telephone call can have a short-term communications advantage. Most people will listen to the caller's introduction. The tracker has the respondent's attention for at least a short period.[10]

What information should be presented during those critical moments? The legitimacy of the person calling and the importance of a response are the two central respondent attitudes that the researcher is trying to influence. The researcher can establish the legitimacy of the tracking request with three pieces of information:

1. The name of the tracker;
2. The name of the sponsoring institution; and
3. Evidence of knowledge about the person sought.

Revealing the tracker's name establishes a personal tone and informs the respondent that the disclosure of a name is not a sensitive issue.[11] The name of the sponsoring institution generalizes the respondent's attitudes about the legitimacy of the institution to the study. The institutional affiliation is important because the researcher does not have time to establish the independent legitimacy of the study or the researcher's identity.

Providing information about the person sought establishes that the tracker has had prior contact with the respondent. Information such as the name of the former high school, the year attended, and the grade reduces confusion about the identity of the panel member sought.

The telephone message must be simple and clear. The key to maintaining simplicity beyond an initial short introduction is for trackers to respond only to questions asked by the respondent. Variations of these four questions are often asked:

1. How did you get my name?
2. Why do you want the address?
3. What is the study about?
4. Where are you phoning from?

Short, rehearsed responses provide information for the respondent to make a decision that is favorable to the study objective.

Often friends or relatives are reluctant to provide address information for fear that the caller will try to force a respondent to continue to participate in the study. We found that telling a parent that we will "invite" or "provide an opportunity" for a son or daughter to continue in the study improved the probability of a favorable response.

Personnel

Tracking reports routinely note the importance of working with well-trained personnel (Freedman, Thornton, and Camburn 1980; Barnes 1972; Homans 1972; Skeels and Skodak 1965; Wilcox 1965). The effect of personnel on tracking is especially evident in attempts to locate hard-to-find respondents. Often an experienced tracker will locate people whom the novice could not find.

Several personality traits warrant consideration as selection criteria for choosing successful trackers:

1. Good interpersonal skills (courteous, tactful, friendly, coherent, able to identify with respondents);
2. Self-confidence;
3. Reliability;
4. Inquisitiveness and creativity (ingenuity, resourcefulness, intuitiveness);
5. Persistence coupled with patience; and
6. Attention to detail in finding leads and logging details of the search.

In addition, special skills such as fluency in a foreign language are important if tracking is conducted on ethnic groups. Barnes (1972) suggests using trackers of the same social class and ethnic origin to avoid arousing suspicion during community visits, though she cautions that trackers selected solely on the basis of ethnic origin may be detrimental if they do not possess the necessary personality traits and skills.

Personal characteristics of trackers may introduce problems. People note accents. Trackers are usually successful in alleviating suspicions, but time is needed to explain why they "sound funny." Respondents are sensitive to a variety of information cues that need to be consistent with the content of the communication. Whether it be ethnic origin, physical appearance, style of dress, or manner of speech, respondents hear and see inconsistencies that typically translate into requests for additional information regarding the legitimacy of the request.

Several acquired capabilities are also important to the success of the tracking effort. A good tracker will quickly develop these:

1. A general knowledge of the study;
2. Experience in the various aspects of the tracking enterprise;
3. Commitment to the success of the study (enthusiasm); and
4. A knowledge of the geographical area in which tracking will take place.

Taken together, these traits and acquired capabilities limit the number of eligible personnel for tracking to a select group. Since the pool of potential personnel is limited, training, supervision, and monitoring are necessary to the success of the tracking enterprise.

Tracker Fatigue and Morale

Tracking is an intense activity, requiring a level of concentration that is difficult to maintain over long periods. A major personnel problem is tracking fatigue. As panel members are located, the residual becomes more difficult and requires more time. Morale may suffer.

Several strategies have been tried to combat tracking fatigue. Clarridge, Sheehy, and Hauser (1977) limited telephone tracking to two-hour periods to maintain tracker efficiency. The researchers assigned those who wished to work longer to other tasks. Another strategy is to use a team approach to tracking (Freedman, Thornton, and Camburn 1980). Like most other group processes, the team approach is inefficient from the standpoint of time, but because of the varied insights of team members, it is effective in locating difficult cases. We found that trackers could work effectively for three or four hours if their activities were varied, they could physically move from their phoning stations, and they were not required to work every day. Variability is also created by assigning trackers to do directory searches, telephone searches, and record keeping for groups of about twenty-five names at a time.

It is easy to maintain morale at the beginning of tracking because success comes easily. Later, however, motivation wanes if there are no incentives to increase trackers' satisfaction with their work. Incentives may be monetary, but it is also possible and useful to modify the project goals. For example, during the early phases when it is easy to locate large numbers of cases, the project director can encourage trackers to find as many people as they can. Competition benefits morale. Supervision at this stage is necessary to ensure that speed does not supplant accuracy and attention to detail. As the effort progresses, the emphasis can change to the percentage of respondents located. When tracking becomes very difficult, it is useful for several trackers jointly to review hard-to-find cases and to exchange information on procedures and experiences. This alters the emphasis from individual effort to group success. We found that location of a particularly difficult person often brought congratulations from other trackers, and positive reinforcement from peers became an incentive. These procedures enable the researcher to maintain morale without increasing supervision.

The procedures for maintaining morale and combating fatigue work best in centralized tracking facilities, but they can also be applied in noncentralized tracking efforts. Newsletters and staff meetings can communicate the same norms if done frequently to compensate for the lack of constant interaction between trackers. Finally, whatever procedures are followed, the need for positive reinforcement cannot be overstated (Freedman, Thornton, and Camburn 1980). In summary, the selection and training of trackers and the maintenance of trackers' morale are critical to the success of the effort.

Location Rates

The telephone approach can be used as the major approach in a tracking strategy or as a supplement following mail or community-visit efforts. The order of approaches affects the location rate because the follow-up approach will apply to the more difficult cases.

Two major panel studies inform our discussion of telephone-tracking situations. The first is the Wisconsin Study (Clarridge, Sheehy, and Hauser 1977), which relied on telephone tracking as the major approach. The second is the National Longitudinal Study of the High School Class of 1972 (Fetters 1974), which used the telephone to supplement a mail approach.

The Wisconsin Study. Sewell and Hauser accomplished one of the most successful large-scale tracking efforts with their seventeen-year follow-up of Wisconsin high school students in 1975. The search tracked 10,317 students who were seniors in 1957.

A restudy of the respondents in 1964, seven years after the initial study, located 87 percent of the original sample. This effort gave trackers some basic identifying information that was no more than ten years old: respondent's name and address in 1964, respondent's parents' names and address in 1964, schools attended since 1957, respondent's and spouse's (if female and married) 1964 occupation, and military experience since 1957.

The researchers divided the sample into ten randomly assigned, equal-sized groups based on sex, socioeconomic status, and mental-ability scores. This was done to allow the tracking effort to terminate short of completion for budget reasons without jeopardizing the random sample. The researchers avoided direct contact with the respondents before the interview to minimize refusals to participate. Whenever possible, they traced respondents through their parents.

From the experience based on one subgroup, Clarridge, Sheehy, and Hauser (1977) report that a telephone-directory search provided leads on 98 percent of the parents. They located 83 percent of the respondents through information provided by parents. They found an additional 10 percent by searching for respondent names in telephone directories. Telephone contacts with employers, college alumni offices, and other post-secondary schools yielded addresses for an additional 4 percent of the subsample. Finally, they used city directories, post offices, and military-locator services to bring the total percentage for the subgroup to 98.6 percent.

The 1975 tracking effort located 97.4 percent of the original respondents. Clarridge and colleagues attribute their success to extensive use of the telephone, to organization and management of the search procedures, to the availability of diverse types of identification on the respondents, to trackers' persistence, and to allocating sufficient funds to accomplish the tracking tasks successfully. We suggest that a carefully formulated research design and attention to detail were additional reasons for their success with the telephone approach.

The National Longitudinal Study of the High School Class of 1972. The Wisconsin Study relied primarily on the telephone approach. The National Longitudinal Study, by comparison, relied on a mail strategy supplemented by telephone.

In the spring of 1972, the National Center for Educational Statistics conducted a study involving a national probability sample of over 21,000 seniors in 1,200 high schools (Fetters 1974). The sample of schools was chosen from a universe that was stratified by seven variables: public-nonpublic, region, enrollment, proximity to college, percentage minority enrollment, income level of community, and degree of urbanization. Four follow-ups were conducted: 1973, 1974, 1976, and 1979.

The respondent information available to trackers varied by successive follow-ups. In 1973 trackers had each respondent's full name, birth date, name of high school, 1972 address taken from school records, and social security number. In 1974 the information included the respondent's full name, 1973 address, name and address of parents, name and address of two other people not living at the respondent's home, name of the respondent's employer, respondent's driver's license number, and name of the post-secondary educational institution attended, where appropriate. In the 1976 follow-up, the information included an update of previous information and the full name of the respondent's spouse, if married.

The project implemented nearly identical tracking procedures for each follow-up (King and Thorne 1977). The procedures began with a newsletter, which enclosed a return postcard for address verification. The newsletter was mailed to the respondent's last-known address.

If a respondent's current address could not be ascertained by mail, the name was assigned to telephone procedures. Trackers in a centralized telephone facility searched nationwide following established procedures, implemented in this order:

1. Telephone calls were placed to parents, guardians, or other close kin requesting respondent's correct address.
2. Contacts were made with one or both of the two individuals listed by the respondent in the first follow-up as people who would always know the respondent's address.
3. Contacts were made with the post-secondary school the respondent attended or planned to attend. If the respondent planned to work, contact was made with the last-known employer.
4. Telephone calls were placed to neighbors or parents of the respondent. Names and telephone numbers were secured through city directories, address-telephone cross-reference directories, chambers of commerce, and public libraries.
5. Contacts were made with the respondent's high school principal, coordinator, teacher, or other school official.
6. Telephone calls were placed with state departments of motor vehicles.
7. Contacts were made with local government agencies (such as registrars of deeds or election boards), requesting a check of records for the name and address of the person or parents.
8. In cases where the respondent was traced to an organization or institution (a prison, the armed services, the Peace Corps, and so on), the researchers telephoned that reference.
9. Local credit bureaus and retail credit companies were contacted to obtain a current address.

The investigators located and interviewed 94 percent of the original participants ($N = 22,654$) in the first follow-up, 92 percent in the second follow-up, and 89 percent in the third. After the fourth follow-up, 82 percent of the original panel members had data available for all four follow-ups.

Information available on the telephone tracking in the first, third, and fourth follow-ups demonstrates the success the researchers experienced in contacting people by telephone. One clerical hour and 6.6 telephone calls per case were required to complete the telephone component of the first follow-up ($N = 1,836$). The average telephone charge was $5.88 per case.[12] Data on the third follow-up indicate that 4,234 cases were assigned to telephone trackers, of which 88 percent were located. About one-half of a clerical hour and two telephone calls were required to locate these respondents (King and Thorne 1977). The telephone procedures in the fourth follow-up located about 96 percent ($N = 6,933$) of the respondents who could not be contacted by mail. An average of 0.56 clerical hours and 2.3 telephone calls were required (King 1981).

The National Longitudinal Study of the High School Class of 1972 and the Wisconsin Study illustrate the tracking success that can be obtained by the telephone approach. Although a few respondents were not found, the telephone approach can result in location rates of over 90 percent.

The Community-Visit Approach

The community-visit approach relies on personal contacts to track panel members. This approach permits a tracker to assess visually which businesses, churches, schools, and houses are in close proximity to the respondent's old address. Neighbors, grocers, pharmacists, clergy, bankers, postal carriers, and others are identified by their physical proximity to a respondent's former address and asked about the respondent's whereabouts. Thus the tracker is not restricted by unpublished telephone numbers.

Local residents have information and social contacts that are available to them but not to outsiders. This information is tapped by establishing a personal rapport with community residents. Personal contact is usually the best method for establishing this rapport and obtaining compliance to a request for help because the tracker's physical presence often increases the cost for not responding.

The disadvantages of the community-visit approach are substantial. The costs are extremely high. There are difficulties in supervising and motivating trackers. There is a potential for physical harm to the tracker. Respondents may be suspicious and fear the tracker. Further, compared to the telephone and mail approaches, the costs of tracking by community visits range from substantial to astronomical as sample size and dispersion increase. Travel costs and personnel time are the major expenses.

Consider, for example, the costs of tracking 125 children and their parents (111 of whom were adopted) after an interval of sixteen to twenty-one years (Skeels and Skodak 1965). The study located 100 percent of the participants, but the investigators personally visited 208 different communities in 24 states and repeated visits as necessary to several larger communities. The investigators spent 309 workdays on 55 separate trips. Travel and per-diem expenses totaled $12,583. The estimated salary cost based on time spent in the field was an additional $18,150. Total costs averaged about $123 per interview. Locating and interviewing would cost $368 per case in 1981 dollars. That means that a study of five thousand respondents would cost $1,840,000 today.

Community visits require independent efforts and considerable initiative by the trackers. Extreme heat and cold, the physical effort of climbing flights of stairs, dogs, and unruly people take their toll on a tracker's enthusiasm to pursue leads. Close supervision is difficult to maintain and may actually repress the tracker's inclination to pursue leads, which is the strength of the method. Maintaining tracker efficiency is much more difficult. Opportunities to review difficult cases and share insights are not part of the normal routine because trackers work independently and have little knowledge of their colleagues' activities. Sole reliance on the community-visit approach requires established procedures for referring leads and an extensive follow-up process to ensure that leads are pursued. Finally, researchers must also consider their liability for the physical well-being of trackers when contemplating the community-visit approach.

We note one other potential problem: trackers can harm property and people. A humorous account is reported by Willits, Crider, and Bealer (1969) on how a researcher backed a car into a farmer's drainage ditch. On a subsequent trip the same investigator noticed his car, which he had parked, rolling down a hill. The alertness of a local garage attendant helped to avert disaster. These accounts are humorous and undoubtedly are the exception. Nonetheless, there is the potential for more serious problems that researchers contemplating community visits should consider.

Some of the disadvantages of the community-visit approach can be lessened with planning. Researchers can lower costs by scheduling a sequence of visits in close proximity to minimize travel time. In practice, however, the rest of the world does not quite operate that way. Families are not home. Former neighbors move to new neighborhoods. People are busy or unwilling to take time to help. The result is that the tracker ends up traveling out of the target neighborhood to check a new lead. Use of the telephone becomes a necessity.

Another way to reduce costs is to pay trackers on a per-locate basis rather than an hourly wage. The advantage is that the researcher can estimate the total cost of community visits because the variables of travel time and search time are fixed. The disadvantage is that trackers may search for only the easy cases and ignore the cases that require more time and effort.

The potential for physical harm is difficult to predict. A schedule that sends women out during the day and men at night is one way to reduce risk (Lewis 1972). Using indigenous and streetwise interviewers may further minimize risk.

Fear and suspicion are more difficult to overcome. The respondent who is afraid will not accommodate the tracker. In some situations, the only communication that occurs may be a quick glance through a peephole to determine whether the caller outside is a police officer, salesperson, social worker, thug, or friend. If the tracker has not established a good rapport in the local area, the tracker will appear as a stranger. The tracker's style of dress and demeanor will in large part determine the attributions made by the respondent.

Location Rates

The best evidence for the effectiveness of community visits is the Rural Pennsylvania Panel Study (Willits, Crider, and Bealer 1969). As part of their design, the investigators sought 320 people using various applications of the mail, telephone, and community-visit approaches. The telephone approach was successful in contacting 82 percent of this subsample. The researchers assumed that anyone contacted by telephone calls to the community could also be contacted by a visit. To augment the limited number not tracked by telephone, they assigned other panel members from the main tracking effort. Thus, the community visits attempted to locate a disproportionate number of hard-to-find cases.

Three separate points of initial contact were evaluated in two different communities. The researchers made contacts at the post office, the high school, and the neighborhood where the respondent attended high school in 1947. Visits made to the community where the respondent lived as a young adult in 1957 started at the post office, with employers, and in the neighborhood.

The location rates for community visits in the 1947 community were 58 percent when the search started at the post office, 73 percent when begun at the high school, and 82 percent when begun in the neighborhood. Searches started in the 1957 community resulted in location rates of 24 percent for the post office visit, 60 percent for the employer visit, and 59 percent for the neighborhood visit. Trackers located most of the respondents after talking with only three to four contact people. Thus, community visits to the rural neighborhood in which the young person lived while attending high school produced four of five young adults who were not located by the telephone approach.

These high location rates may be applicable only to rural areas where extensive social contacts exist, however. Willits, Crider, and Bealer report that neighbors in large cities such as Philadelphia or in small towns were generally cordial and knowledgeable, but the response rate dropped from 82 percent in rural areas in 1947 to 59 percent in 1957 when some of the respondents migrated to more urban areas.

In summary, community visits are useful for locating people who do not have telephones, are hard-to-locate, or are members of special populations that require personal contact. In small studies it is possible to achieve a high success rate but at high costs. In large studies the costs are prohibitive except for limited applications to special situations.

Comparison of Tracking Approaches

There is a lack of empirical data upon which to make comparative statements and base conclusions about the tracking approaches. Many studies provide overall descriptions of procedures followed. A few count the number of information sources used. But only one, to our knowledge, made a comparison of the relative effectiveness of tracking approaches. Using a special subsample of former rural high school students, Willits, Crider, and Bealer (1969) made contact with about 51 percent by mail, 82 percent by telephone, and 78 percent by community visit.[13] However, generalizing this experience and tracking efficiency to people from urban backgrounds is probably not warranted.

We draw on our own and the reported experiences of others to summarize and compare the characteristics of the approaches. Table 3-1 presents a summary comparison of the three tracking approaches we discussed. For purposes of comparison, we apply the approaches to the following hypothetical circumstances. We assume a panel size of two thousand to five thousand participants. We assume that the target panel is heterogeneous and representative of the general population. We assume that automated printing equipment, computer facilities, and well-trained personnel are available. Finally, we assume that a moderate amount of identifying information is known about the respondents.

Table 3-1 illustrates three general conclusions. First, community visits may be most successful where the design requires personal contact and tracking flexibility, but they are difficult to supervise, time-consuming, and expensive.

Second, a mail approach costs less, but the anticipated tracking success is also lower. The small number of personnel required to operate a centralized facility makes the mail approach the easiest to monitor and control, but what is gained in control is lost in search flexibility. The postal carrier and postal regulations determine who can and cannot be contacted.

Table 3-1
Comparison of Tracking Approaches on Five Outcome Criteria

	Evaluation Criteria				
Approach	Personalization[a]	Search Flexibility[b]	Supervisory Control[c]	Tracking Speed[d]	Tracking Cost[e]
Community Visit	***	***	*	*	*
Telephone	**	**	**	***	**
Mail	*	*	***	**	***

Note: *** = produces most favorable outcome; ** = produces favorable outcome; * = produces least favorable outcome.

[a]The extent to which the researcher can tailor the contact to fit the situation.

[b]The extent to which information sources such as relatives, neighbors, and friends can be identified and contacted.

[c]The extent to which investigators can monitor personnel and coordinate tracking effort.

[d]The amount of time it takes to track at least 55 percent of the panel members.

[e]The average cost for locating a panel member.

Third, the telephone approach is a compromise on these comparison criteria. It is more personal than mail contact but less personal than a visit, less flexible for identifying information sources than community visits but more flexible than mail contact, and considerably less costly than community visits but significantly more expensive than mail. The telephone is the most efficient in terms of speed. If telephone numbers are available, researchers can contact respondents across the country with ease.

As panel size and dispersion increase, respondent characteristics vary dramatically. Typically this requires that the researcher combine and sequence approaches. Cost then becomes a primary consideration. The researcher is left with limited options. The panel study can be conducted knowing that resources must be spread thinly and that attrition will be severe. Alternatively, the researcher can reduce panel size and, by concentrating resources and increasing tracking options, reduce attrition for the smaller subsample.

The following applications represent the role each approach can play separately or in combination in a tracking design:

1. Community visits are best suited for intensive tracking of a small number of hard-to-locate respondents.
2. The mail approach is the most effective for general screening of the easy-to-locate.
3. The telephone approach is the workhorse for locating the typical, mobile panel member.

The role of the three approaches is determined largely by the access that trackers have to information sources. As more information is available to the researcher, the telephone approach becomes less costly and has a comparative advantage over the mail and community-visit approaches.

Notes

1. In some instances the post office forwards third-class mail within a city. Usually, however, postal workers discard the material without notification to the sender.

2. The addressee must file a change-of-address form with the post office. The post office will forward mail to the new address for a period of one year. The following year the address can be obtained from the post office for a fee. After two years the post office destroys the address record.

3. The researcher can take advantage of the lowest postal rates for Business Reply Mail by establishing a deposit account. A 78 percent response must be obtained before using stamped, return envelopes becomes less expensive than using the current business reply rate. Failure to establish a

deposit account lowers the cost advantage considerably. If more than 50 percent respond using a business reply envelope not covered by a deposit account, then using postage stamps is less expensive than using business reply envelopes.

4. Up to thirty-six average-length letters can be produced per minute.

5. The total design perspective is based on an exchange theory rationale for respondent behavior. The method has achieved higher response rates than those typically reported in mail questionnaire efforts.

6. Anne S. Ishler and Dan E. Moore presented the findings of this study in a panel discussion at the 1980 annual meetings of the Rural Sociological Association.

7. The nonpersonalized treatment used a large outgoing envelope. Attention was drawn to the logo, "The Citizen's Viewpoint," by bordering the logo with heavy lines.

8. Most mailings were sent by third-class mail.

9. See the section on telephone directory assistance in chapter 4.

10. Groves and Kahn (1979) note that instances of people hanging up the telephone immediately after an introduction occur most often when trackers call people in metropolitan areas.

11. Care should be exercised to avoid the possibility of harassment by respondents, particularly if calls are placed locally. Sexual overtures from male respondents to female trackers occur. We observed that respondents invoked reciprocity norms to try to obtain trackers' telephone numbers and addresses. The standard line was, "I'll tell you his address if you'll tell me yours." Trackers can usually satisfy these reactions by providing the project telephone number and address.

12. These figures are based on internal reports that the Research Triangle Institute provided to the authors.

13. These are average location rates for the 1947 and 1957 telephone and community-visit approaches. The community-visit search included a large number of hard-to-locate people.

4

Tracking
Information Sources

The number of information sources that a tracker can access limits the search for a respondent. For most people there are various sources for a current address. Many are obvious; the general public uses them daily. Other sources are not widely known or commonly used but nonetheless are valuable for locating mobile people.

The first part of this chapter presents a summary of the main sources of information that past studies used to locate addresses for respondents. We do not include a discussion of special information sources available to locate former prisoners, mental health clients, the physically impaired, the aged, and other special populations. These special sources may be unique to particular areas. Some are used to track special populations only or are difficult for most researchers to access. They cannot provide the basis for typical tracking strategies and therefore are not discussed.

We orient our comments to tracking young adults for two reasons. First, most major panel studies involve tracking respondents who were high school students at the time of original data collection. The second wave typically gathers information from them in their early careers. Second, we are most familiar with the information sources we used to track people age 28 to 31.

Many articles reviewing information sources were published prior to the 1974 privacy regulations so some reassessment of the earlier conclusions is required. In most instances the legislation does not eliminate use of information sources but does regulate the conditions of access to information.

Some information sources are more successful than others in gaining contact with a respondent. The second part of this chapter examines the relative effectiveness of the information sources. The National Longitudinal Surveys and Project Talent provide indications of the level of success that might be expected from the various sources. The National Longitudinal Surveys employed a community-visit approach. Project Talent relied on a centralized telephone approach to track a special subsample of nonrespondents.

The limitations of reported data do not permit statements about the relative success of each source of information for tracking particular types of respondents. The Rural Pennsylvania Panel Study (Willits, Crider, and Bealer 1969) explored how many respondents could be located from nine different information sources. Their procedures compared information approaches but did not establish the superiority of any one source for all tracking situations. The third part of this chapter organizes the information sources into a hierarchy based on the hypothetical effectiveness of approaches.

Information Sources

Following is a description of fifteen sources of information that researchers commonly use in telephone and community-visit approaches. We base our comments on published articles, unpublished reports, training manuals, communications with study directors, and our own experience with the Career Development Study.

Family and Relatives

Family and relatives are the most likely to know the current address of a respondent or of someone else who knows the address.

There are several ways to identify relatives. For respondents who reported a home address during their high-school years, about 55 percent of the parents can be contacted at the same address more than a decade later (Temme 1975). If the parents moved, it is easier to locate the family by contacting residents and neighbors at the old address than to try to contact the respondent at a more recent address (Willits, Crider, and Bealer 1969). Parents are more established in their careers and have more social contacts in their community than do young adults. They are also less mobile.

Contacts with other community members—postal personnel, teachers, clergy, and druggists—may identify someone who knows the family. Another method for identifying relatives is to telephone people listed as having the same last name as the respondent in telephone or city directories (Eckland 1968). In many cases, calls to people with the same last name quickly produces a relative. If a tracker calls a person who is not a relative of the respondent, it is useful to ask that person to identify the other names listed in the telephone directory that are his or her relatives and therefore are not likely to be relatives of the person sought.

Parents and relatives usually cooperate. A few parents refuse or cannot provide a current address. There are many reasons for refusals. The parent may feel that surveys are useless. A parent or relative may protect kin for legal, health, financial, or domestic reasons. In some situations a parent will state why an address cannot be given. A more common reply is, "My child would not be interested in that." In a few circumstances the response is "He's away," "He's working out of town," "I do not know where she is right now, but she will probably be back in a few months," or "He's out of the country." Homans (1972) reports that such statements are likely indicators that the respondent is in jail. We found that discrepant information from various family members occasionally indicates that the respondent is in jail.

Attempts by parents or relatives to deflect contact with respondents should not be interpreted as a refusal by the respondent. Many sons or daughters are very cooperative when found (Temme 1975). Of course, the opposite—willing parents but unwilling respondents—also occurs. The only way to determine if a respondent will participate is to ask that person directly.

Lack of family cooperation is difficult to work around because families are the easiest way to establish contact with mobile respondents. Moreover, relatives usually refer trackers to family members if they do not have the respondent's current address. We failed to contact 23 percent of the 126 respondents not located because family members refused to provide a current address.

Fathers are more protective than mothers, and they are also less sure of a son or daughter's whereabouts. A father who has been asked for address information will usually ask the mother. Experienced trackers ask to speak to the mother if the father answers the telephone.

Neighbors

Neighbors are good information sources unless a person changes residence frequently. Neighbors generally know the names of children, where parents work, names of close friends, and where the family moved.

Skeels and Skodak (1965) recount a visit to a community to locate a respondent who was adopted into a family that had one daughter. A former neighbor remembered the daughter's name and that she married a young man named Ralph Strand. The neighbor remembered that the Strands moved to Des Moines, Iowa, and lived on Fourth Street Place. The researchers tried to contact Mr. Strand, but he was not home. Strand's neighbor, however, advised the investigators of his work schedule, his divorce, his former mother-in-law's name prior to her remarriage, her present employer, and her current married name and address. Since the investigators were trying to find Strand's former wife to learn of the adopted daughter's whereabouts, the information about the former mother-in-law provided by the neighbor was valuable.

The extent of knowledge about a family in a neighborhood depends on the type of residence and neighborhood interaction patterns. In urban areas with mostly single-family dwellings, knowledge about a family decreases as the distance between the residences increases. People who live next door or across the street usually know more than those who live farther away. People in the apartments living close to the respondent may know the respondent's whereabouts, but a resident manager may have had more contact with the respondent and have more information about where the respondent moved.

A city directory will identify neighbors of the respondent. If a street-name directory is not available, it may be necessary to call or visit the community to reconstruct the residence pattern. If visits to the neighborhood cannot be made, it may be useful to contact people who may remember the family or identify others who know about the family: local grocers, pharmacists, beauty salon operators, fire station personnel, clergy, post office employees, school personnel, and long-time community residents.

There is little evidence to indicate the tracking effectiveness of telephoning neighbors other than reports stating that it was productive but time-consuming (Clarridge, Sheehy, and Hauser 1977). When a neighbor can be identified, a telephone call to the neighbor usually provides the same information as a community visit.

Former Classmates

Researchers occasionally request the names of a respondent's best friends during data collection, information that provides quick access to the friendship network. Past tracking practice has been to include names of hard-to-find respondents along with questionnaires sent to panel members. The rate of response to these requests for information is low, but information provided is usually useful (Clarridge, Sheehy, and Hauser 1977). Temme (1975) found about 5 percent of his panel members through this procedure.

After confirming that a person is the panel member sought, it is useful to ask immediately for that respondent's help with four or five other names, a procedure with several advantages. First, the respondent may know the whereabouts of a particular panel member. Second, switching the focus of the telephone call or visit to other people shifts a general conversation to a specific topic. Once the list of names is discussed, the tracker has a natural point to terminate the conversation. Finally, eliciting the respondent's aid in a simple task is a foot in the door for cooperation at a later date (Freedman and Fraser 1972).

High School Reunion Committees

One of the most effective alternatives to a community visit is enlisting the assistance of a high school class-reunion committee. Ten- and twenty-year reunions are common. Five-year reunions sometimes occur. Class-reunion committees are reasonably successful in locating their classmates.

The committee members are good sources of information. They recall their own experiences in trying to notify classmates about the reunion. They may work at a bank, insurance company, or other business where they have access to records indicating the whereabouts of a person or relative.

The committee usually develops an address list or file on each classmate and issues a printed program for the reunion. Biographical sketches sometimes include spouses names and places of employment. The reunion committee, whose members are usually long-time community residents, offer the researcher the benefit of a community search at minimal cost.

Our experience is that committees tap the obvious sources of information but often are not aware of or do not make the effort to pursue other sources of information. Thus, the information from a reunion list is likely to be biased toward the less mobile. Nonetheless, reasonably current addresses can be obtained for about 50 percent of a high school class from reunion lists.

Employers

Company records usually include the name of a person to contact in case of an emergency affecting the employee, the employee's social security number, birth date and birthplace, residence address, and the name of a close relative. Forwarding addresses are also sometimes included. In addition, company personnel may identify a respondent's former co-workers and supervisors.

In small companies, access to such information is usually not an issue. The owner, supervisor, or co-worker may recall the former employee and provide a current address or the name of someone who knows it.

Access to information about a former employee may be more difficult in large companies, however. A common response is that personnel records are confidential. Sometimes a large company will identify the respondent's former supervisors. If permission is not given to talk with the supervisor, the personnel department usually will agree to forward a letter to the respondent.

Employer information is an efficient information source. The current address of respondents can be found with additional searching for about 60 percent of the persons sought (Willits, Crider, and Bealer 1969). About 80 percent of the people located through employers require no more than three additional contacts with people mentioned by the employer to locate the respondent.

Knowledge of former employers is useful for determining friendship networks and the possible whereabouts of a respondent. It also provides information concerning the probability that the respondent appears on union, professional society, and licensing agency records (Clarridge, Sheehy, and Hauser 1977).

High Schools

High school halls and classrooms are a major arena for adolescent activities (Coleman 1961). Teachers, secretaries, principals, coaches, counselors, club advisers, and classmates interacted daily with the respondent in high school. School records listed background information, school behavior, and academic performance. Each yearbook published the respondent's activities. By the time the person left high school, a wealth of information accumulated about that person.

The major problem with school information is access. Federal regulations establish conditions under which school records can be released (Office of the Federal Register 1979). This legislation allows access to directory information, which includes such items as the student's name, address, telephone number, date and place of birth, dates of attendance, and name of the most recent school attended. There is, however, considerable state and local variation in the information that is available through the schools. Local educational institutions may define all or none of the directory information as information available to the public.

Access to high school information is problematic, yet most high school principals will help if the goals and benefits of the study are explained. Only one Washington high school in twenty-five that we contacted refused to provide information. We did not find that privacy laws eliminated the high school as a source of information, as did the Wisconsin researchers.[1]

School yearbooks may be difficult to obtain. High schools may retain a copy but are reluctant to lend it. If a copy is not available through the high school, a respondent who attended the school may be more accommodating. Our experience is that females are more likely to keep yearbooks and that respondents are more likely to loan the yearbook if the researcher will pay for certified mail and promise to return it promptly.

A yearbook provides the full name of the respondent and gives clues to the clubs and activities in which the respondent participated. Some yearbooks include names of class advisers and faculty members who may be useful contact sources.

College Registrar, Student Information,
and Alumni Associations

A college registrar's office, student information, and alumni association all maintain records on college students. Applications for enrollment and transcript information are generally kept by the registrar until the student graduates or leaves. At some later time, the file is destroyed, and only the transcript is retained.

Although much of the information on college and university applications and transcripts provides important facts about the respondent, federal regulations prohibit registrars from disclosing nondirectory information without written permission from the former student. There is wide latitude in what constitutes directory information, just as there are numerous interpretations of what constitutes public and private information. If the registrar's office cannot help, a check with a college student information service can quickly verify a possible current registration and current address. The college student directory service is preferable to the printed student directory because it is more current.

University alumni associations are a useful source for current information on students who have graduated. Almost all alumni associations place limits on who can use their address lists, but an explanation of the research purposes of the inquiry is usually sufficient to ensure cooperation. Nonetheless, some colleges provide current addresses only to other alumni or current university employees. In a few instances an alumni office may refuse to provide any information. When a refusal occurs, it is sometimes useful to ask if some advice can be given concerning which telephone directory the researcher might consult. This information may be given.

Coverage is the biggest limitation to alumni records. Some alumni associations list only those who graduated. In the Career Development Study 70 percent (77 percent male, 63 percent female) of the sample attended a two- or four-year college or university within thirteen years after leaving high school. Of those who attended college, 63 percent of the males and 54 percent of the females received a degree. Thus, about half of all who enrolled (one-third of the full sample) would eventually appear on alumni lists of graduates. Even with this coverage limitation, an alumni association is a major source of information about the current addresses of former college students.

Churches

About 68 percent of the U.S. population holds church membership (American Institute of Public Opinion 1978). About 56 percent of these claim to be active members. During an average week about 42 percent of the U.S. population attends church. Most churches maintain membership records. By contacting churches and synagogues in close proximity to the respondent's last-known address, the researcher can check whether the respondent held membership. If the respondent was an active member, the clergy may have personal knowledge about the respondent's family or be able to identify people with whom the respondent associated.

Telephone Directories

The researcher can obtain a telephone directory for almost every community in the United States for a nominal fee. Arrangements can be made at the business office of a local telephone company. If the researcher does not have space to store a large number of telephone directories, microfiche copies, which may be easier to use, are available on a subscription basis.[2] Coverage ranges from the ten largest metropolitan areas in the United States to all areas of 25,000 or more population.

In addition, a researcher may purchase a hard-copy street-address record. The service is contracted on a yearly basis, and the record must be returned at the end of the contract period. The street-address record lists all addresses in a metropolitan area and provides corresponding names and telephone numbers for that address. Unpublished telephone numbers are included in the street-address record.

There are four limitations to telephone directories in tracking. First, directories are four to six weeks out of date when printed and may be two to three months old by the time they are distributed. Telephone companies differ on when they update the directories, and current directories may be dated by as much as a year. Second, not every household has a telephone. Studies indicate that about 90 percent of all households have a telephone (Groves and Kahn 1979). Thus, reliance on telephones introduces some bias.

Second, telephone directories are further limited in that they do not contain unlisted or unpublished numbers. About 20 percent of the U.S. population has unlisted or unpublished telephone numbers. An even higher percentage of unlisted numbers occurs in metropolitan areas (Glasser and Metzger 1975). Third, the first- and middle-name listings in telephone directories are often initials. This is especially the case for single women. Widows sometimes continue to list their husband's name or precede their husband's name with "Mrs." Finding a married female's telephone number is difficult if the listing appears in the husband's name. Fourth, although it is sometimes useful to track mobile people's moves using old directories, there are few archives of telephone directories.[3]

Telephone directories facilitate other tracking techniques, however. For example, the researcher can sometimes locate a relative by placing calls to people with the same last name as a respondent. Directories can also be used to determine a father's or respondent's full name by searching for the same last name and address. However, care must be taken to avoid attributing a brother's, sister's, or relative's name to a respondent, mother, or father.

City and Community Directories

City and community directories are a valuable asset to tracking. Perhaps the best known directory for large cities and towns, published by the R.L. Polk Company, covers more than fourteen hundred cities and suburban areas. Directories are also available for many rural areas.[4]

Directories provide a wealth of information. In addition to information about businesses and churches, Polk directories provide the full name of each person living in the city, the spouse's name if married, names of children over age 18 who are students, the complete street address, a telephone number, a person's occupation and employer, an indication of whether the person owns or rents the residence, and other information that may be useful, such as names of church pastors and business ownership. The directories are arranged by street name and telephone number. If, for example, a person's former address is known, the current resident at that address and neighbors are easily identified in the street-to-name listing. A directory printed for the year prior to the respondent's last-known address provides identification of neighbors at the time the respondent lived in the neighborhood.[5]

The telephone-to-name listing permits the tracker to associate an address with a known telephone number. The tracker can identify a possible address for verification by telephone if a telephone number is known. This feature of city directories is particularly useful for locating people who are cohabiting and are sometimes reluctant to give their address. The researcher can sidestep this reluctance by asking the respondent to verify the address rather than to provide an address.

City directories are useful in other ways. Telephone numbers and addresses that do not appear in a telephone directory and are not provided by directory assistance may be published in a city directory. Further, city directories tend to list the full name of females, a practice that assists in narrowing the search when identical names appear in telephone directories.

As with most other sources of tracking information, access is the largest problem in using a city directory. The first problem is to identify the directories that serve the area in which the researcher believes most respondents live. Local libraries and the chamber of commerce can assist. Once these areas are identified, there are several ways to gain access to the directory information. One can purchase the directories, use a public library or reference copy at the chamber of commerce, or telephone a library or chamber of commerce and request information for a specific listing. Whether the last service is provided varies by locality. Because the person filling the request is not likely to be a trained and experienced tracker, the researcher cannot assume that all available or useful information is provided.

Purchasing current city directories for major cities in which a large number of panel members may be living is a practical investment. Recent editions of city directories can sometimes be obtained through book dealers. Libraries may archive out-of-print directories as reference volumes that are not available for purchase.[6]

Telephone Directory Assistance

The absence of a listing in a telephone directory does not mean information is not available. The most current information on a respondent is available from telephone directory assistance. It is usually quite simple to obtain current information on one or two people. During high-use periods, however, operators are less likely to accommodate requests for additional information or requests for more than two or three listings.[7] Avoidance of peak-use times increases the likelihood that an operator will provide tracking help.

The amount of information the operator has and telephone company rules regulate the amount of information available to the researcher. Willits, Crider, and Bealer (1969) suggest how to be successful in using directory assistance. First, the tracker must remember that all directory-assistance calls are automatically timed and that a random number of calls are monitored by supervisors to evaluate operator adherence to company rules, customer relations, and the adequacy of the information provided. Maximum cooperation from an operator will occur only if the tracker stays within the rule structure imposed on the operator.

Second, directory assistance is designed to provide telephone numbers. Thus a request for a telephone number must be made or the operator will refuse to provide an address. After a telephone number is provided, the question, "Is that still on Central Street?" frequently will bring a reply from the operator that the person lives on a different street. To avoid asking for more detail, we find that providing a house number and a street name will usually result in a reply correcting both the number and the name. If the address is not correct, the operator will likely respond, "No, I show such and such an address." During high-use periods, operators will decline to provide an address or will provide only the street name. The researcher can determine whether the refusal to provide an address was dictated by a busy work load or company policies by calling the same directory-assistance number in the early evening.

If there are rules against releasing listed addresses, one recourse is to telephone directory assistance during the early evening, to ask the operator for help in locating someone, and to explain briefly why the person is sought. An explanation of what is needed and a request for help provides the operator with a reason to use discretion in deciding whether to provide the requested service.

Third, the extent that an operator will search for a listing when an exact town or first name cannot be provided depends on how busy the operator is and the uniqueness of the name of the person for whom a listing is sought.

There are additional considerations in dealing with information operators. The telephone company conveys an image of total accuracy, but operators are not infallible, and some are not reliable.[8] An operator's report of no listing is not definitive when there is information suggesting that a person lives in a particular city. Another call to directory assistance will almost always connect with a different operator, who may find a listing.

Unpublished numbers present special problems for trackers. If a city directory does not list a telephone number, the tracker has no way to check quickly that the person for whom an address is available is the panel member sought. Telephone information centers differ in their policies regarding unpublished numbers. In some centers, an unpublished number is not provided to the operators. In others, operators have access to unpublished information but cannot give the telephone number or address to a caller. Sometimes, an operator may confirm that an address does or does not match the unpublished address for the name a researcher gives to the operator; however, this is not a standard practice, and only a few operators will comply with the request to verify an unpublished address.

Directory assistance can also be used to supply limited geographical information. For example, suppose an address is available for a respondent who lives in a very small town in a state covered by two or three area codes. If the tracker cannot find the small town on a map, a call to each of the directory-assistance numbers will identify in which area the town is located and which directory to consult for listings. Since most people in small towns are acquainted with other residents, the researcher can request assistance from a bank or a church.

List service is a little-known service provided by directory assistance. For a nominal fee, directory assistance can take a written list of names and addresses and provide a current name-address-telephone number listing for each name provided appropriate arrangements are made with a local business office. The search requires only that the name and city be supplied. However, the lack of additional address information for people with common last names may make identification of the person sought problematic. The service permits a researcher to check address and telephone information without making staff arrangements in-house to accomplish the task. The corrected listing will be the most current listing available.

Post Office

People sometimes suggest that one talk to the post office when inquiring about the location of a person because they assume that postal employees can freely give out current address information. That assumption is unfounded. Up to one year after receipt of a forwarding request, the post office will forward first-class mail. The following year, the post office will return the mail to the sender but will keep the address on file for those who request and pay for the information. The researcher must either mail a letter requesting an address correction or fill out a form requesting the new address and pay the fee to obtain an address that has been on file fewer than two years. After two years local post offices discard all forwarding address information.

These postal regulations appear to set limits on the amount of information available from the post office. Yet the experiences of Willits, Crider, and Bealer (1969) and Clarridge, Sheehy, and Hauser (1977) demonstrate that rural post offices are in fact quite helpful. Rural postal employees often recall the whereabouts of particular families and are reasonably willing to assist. In most cases, rural postal workers refer the tracker to friends and relatives who have the address or will forward a letter to the person.

The Rural Pennsylvania Panel Study (Willits, Crider, and Bealer 1969) examined the effectiveness of seeking addresses from a post office. The post office provided current addresses for 38 percent of the people sought. Most of the addresses were obtained from friends and relatives in the community after a postal worker informed the tracker whom to contact. The investigators found that 58 percent could be located by contacting the post office in the community where the family had lived more than twenty years earlier. In contrast, only about 24 percent of the people were located by contact with the post office in the community where the respondent had lived ten years earlier. A substantial amount of time had passed since the families had moved from rural communities. Yet the post office in rural areas helped contact more of the families than were contacted by visits to the post offices in the urban community in which the respondent lived more recently.

In summary, contacting a post office is not likely to result in high tracking success, particularly in large cities. Postal workers in rural areas can often direct trackers to friends and relatives in the community who may know the respondent's or family's whereabouts. Recent efforts to close rural stations could alter these outcomes dramatically.

Driver's License Registration

Eighty-five percent of all U.S. citizens age 16 and over have a current driver's license (U.S. Department of Commerce 1980b). This wide coverage of names, addresses, and related information in a public file makes driver's license registration a useful source of tracking information. State regulations vary with respect to the amount of information that is included in the file and the extent to which the information is public.

There are several problems in using driver's license files for tracking. The license-renewal period determines how often and when the addresses are updated. Some people comply with requirements to change licenses with address changes, probably because of the utility of the operator's license for identification purposes and the potential problems of using an expired license. Others wait until their old license expires before renewing at a new address. Nonresident students are often not required to obtain an in-state license. Thus, the address listed on a driver's license may or may not be current. However, minimally the tracker can find out where the respondent once lived.

Most states require that the researcher request a driver's record in writing, although telephone and over-the-counter service may also be provided. The driver's name and date of birth or the driver's license number is usually required to initiate a search. In a sample of six states, the charge for the information ranged from seventy-five cents to five dollars. A two dollar charge was the most frequent. The service typically required from ten days to two weeks.

Driver's license registrations provide an unobtrusive way to obtain reasonably current addresses or to have a letter forwarded to a respondent. Whether state offices have sufficient personnel to handle a large number of requests and whether they will provide an address or just forward mail varies by state.

Voter Registration Files

Voter registration files are public records that contain names and current addresses. Previous addresses, place of birth, birth date, phone number, and other information may be included.

The information is usually current, but there are several difficulties in accessing the information. First, the records are not centralized. In most states voter registration records are maintained at the county level. Second, most county registration offices have small staffs and are not equipped to handle large numbers of requests. Most offices are able to handle only two or three names per written or verbal request. A third problem is access from a distance. In most counties, the records are open to the public for inspection, but a request by telephone or mail introduces potential roadblocks. For example, a county clerk in Minnesota stated that the records are for use only for political or law enforcement purposes. He remarked that the restriction is seldom applied to people who personally inspect the records but is frequently applied to those who write or telephone requesting information.

A fourth problem is coverage. Mobile individuals are less likely to register to vote than are long-term residents. Over 80 percent of people who do not move for six or more years are registered to vote compared to only 54 percent of those living in a residence for one year or less (U.S. Department of Commerce 1978). Thus, voter registration provides current information on a large number of people who do not move often. Access to the records is difficult, especially for large tracking efforts. However, it may be advisable to search voter registration records in tracking situations where it is likely that a large number of panel members are living in the same county.

Military Locator Services

Military locator services assist in the location of military personnel. Requests to use locator services require the following information in writing:

1. Service member's full name;
2. Current rank or rating;
3. Social security number, military identification number, or parents' full names and the service member's date and place of birth;
4. Last-known address or other information that uniquely identifies the person sought;
5. Relationship of the person making the request to service member; and
6. Reason for requesting the current address.

Items 1 through 4 provide the required information, but locator service personnel indicate that it may be possible to locate a person by means of the full name only. A social security number or military identification number eases the search procedure and increases the likelihood that the locator services will honor the request.

A response from the locator service usually takes one to two weeks. A request for the address of a retiree is generally forwarded directly to that person. If the person is no longer in the service, notice is given, but a current address is not provided.

Locator services are available for each branch of the military. To submit a request, a letter should be sent to the appropriate branch of service.[9]

Other Sources of Information

Other sources of information can be used to search for people who are difficult to locate. Realtors, utility companies, city and county clerks and assessors, and city planning and engineering offices can sometimes provide information about the owner or renter of a residence.

Professional associations and unions keep records of people licensed to practice certain professions. College sororities and fraternities maintain records of past and current members. Many people are members of community-service organizations. The researcher can examine microfilm copies of old newspapers for vital statistics and human-interest stories. The researcher can list the names of people who have not yet been located in local newspapers and request information about them.[10] Public libraries, the local chamber of commerce, and city planning and engineering offices have directories and other information about the local community. Maps from libraries or from city planning and engineering offices are often useful in determining changes in residential areas.

Local school districts conduct a school census that aids the location of school-age respondents or their parents. State agencies maintain birth, death, and marriage records that are useful though expensive and difficult to access. Records such as marriage licenses, real estate records, and wills are not particularly valuable sources of information for tracking because only a small proportion of the respondents can be located through them (Willits, Crider, and Bealer 1969).

Some organizations will track people for a fee. Temme (1975), for example, paid local high school honor societies and parent-teacher associations to locate respondents who had attended local schools. Equifax (formerly Retail Credit Bureau) and Tracers Company of America are commercial companies that specialize in locating and contacting people. Equifax located about two-thirds of 423 hard-to-find twelfth graders referred by Project Talent (Rossi et al. 1976). Equifax also located twelve out of fifty ninth graders who could not be located by Project Talent staff.

Tracers Company of America, based in New York City, provides the same services. The company is reputed to be competitive in fees and efficient at finding people (Eckland 1968). It has a two-tier fee structure with a search initiation fee for each case submitted and a contingency fee for each case located.

In summary, tracking requires resourcefulness, imagination, and persistence. Resourcefulness involves taking full advantage of information sources that are obvious and readily available. Imagination involves going beyond the obvious and tapping the hidden sources. Persistence involves leaving no stone unturned until each respondent is located.

Effectiveness of Information Sources

What response rates can one anticipate from using the various information sources? The National Longitudinal Surveys and the Project Talent special surveys provide some indication.

The National Longitudinal Surveys

The U.S. Census Bureau conducted the National Longitudinal Surveys in a series of studies between 1966 and 1978. The bureau faced the problems of retaining respondents in samples over a period of years and establishing the most effective means of relocating respondents for follow-up interviews (Fondelier 1976).

Four population groups were surveyed: the Mature Men's Survey of respondents who were 45 to 59 years old in 1966 ($N = 5,020$); the Mature Women's Survey of respondents who were 30 to 44 years old in 1966 ($N = 5,083$); the Young Men's Survey of respondents who were 14 to 24 in 1966 ($N = 5,225$); and the Young Women's Survey of respondents who were 14 to 24 years old in 1968 ($N = 5,159$). The samples were of the national civilian population for specific age cohorts in the period 1966 to 1968. Follow-up interviews were conducted at one- or two-year intervals over a ten-year period, and careful records were kept of the methods used to relocate respondents in each sample over time.

Census staff provided interviewers with considerable information about the respondent: the name and address of each respondent; the respondent's telephone number; all addresses at which the respondent had lived over the period of the study; the names of all persons who had lived with the respondent since the study began; names and addresses of present and past employers since the study began; the names of colleges attended, if any; and the names, addresses, and telephone numbers of two persons who would always know where the respondent could be reached. Interviewers were authorized to contact other sources for locating respondents, including the post office, local businesses, the telephone company, and persons living in the area. Case records were kept.

Fondelier (1976) selected one year from each of the surveys to examine closely the relative effectiveness of the methods used: the 1970 Young Men's Survey, the 1970 Young Women's Survey, the 1969 Mature Women's Survey, and the 1971 Mature Men's Survey. The following procedures were used in these surveys:

1. The postal service verified respondents' addresses a few months before interviewing began.
2. An interviewer visited the verified address.
3. If direct contact with the respondent was not made, interviewers were instructed to use the most convenient of the following methods for acquiring additional information: contact current residents of the house, landlord or manager, neighbors, persons listed as probably knowing where the respondent would be, schools, post offices, directory-assistance operators, and search telephone directories.
4. When direct contact was made, the interviewer recorded all methods used to relocate the person.

The study design was less than rigorous, and its limitations must be considered when interpreting the results. As Fondelier notes, the limitations are not trivial. First, the application of tracking methods was not randomized. Rather, trackers followed their individual preferences in choosing the primary approach they used and the order of follow-up approaches.

Second, because the trackers worked subjectively, the tracking methods were not used equally. Not every method was used to try to locate respondents who were never located. One method was used as little as 1.3 percent of the time (contacting the school in the Mature Men's Survey) whereas another was used as much as 28.5 percent of the time (contacting persons listed as knowing where the respondent would be in the Young Men's Survey).

Third, the findings are based on methods used to locate the respondents who were found and completed the interview. People who were not relocated or not interviewed are not part of the data base. These are serious methodological deficiencies that cast the findings in the form of hypotheses yet to be tested rather than as conclusions to guide future research.

The findings suggest that asking the respondent during the initial study to identify people who would likely know their current address is a successful procedure. Of 1,590 contacts with people who would likely know where the respondent was living later, 69 percent resulted in a current address for the respondent. The trackers tried to gain the same information by talking with the occupant of the respondent's old residence, former neighbors, and former apartment managers but were successful in learning the respondent's whereabouts only 20 percent of the time. People who lived in the respondent's neighborhood were much less likely to know the respondent's new addresss than were friends and relatives who lived several or many miles away. The results seem to highlight the importance of knowing or obtaining the names of parents, relatives, friends, and employers. These appear to be the most effective sources of information that aid location of the respondent.

Project Talent

The most ambitious tracking effort thus far attempted was Project Talent, which drew an original probability sample representative of all U.S. high school students in grades nine through twelve in 1960 ($N = 375,122$). Special-interest samples of fifteen-year-olds and other students from selected schools increased the initial sample to a total of about 400,000 people. Periodic follow-up surveys were done at one, five, and eleven years following the expected year of graduation from high school.

Personal information on each respondent informed the tracking effort: respondent's full name, address, birth date, school attended, father's complete name, and mother's maiden name. In addition, Project Talent tried to maintain addresses over the years by sending an annual newsletter that included requests for changes of address from the respondent and the postal service. The eleven-year follow-up for the four grade levels located and interviewed from 20 to 29 percent of the panel members (Rossi et al. 1976).

Project Talent attempted to compensate for the substantial attrition by applying an elaborate weighting scheme for the respondent data. Staff made an intensive effort to track a subsample of the original respondents in order to establish the weights. A number of procedures were followed by the in-house staff to locate these special nonrespondents:

1. A search was conducted from the information sheets on file for each respondent.
2. Telephone directories were checked.
3. Directory-assistance operators were contacted.
4. Schools were contacted.
5. Marriage records and department of motor vehicle records were searched.

Project Talent put differential reliance on in-house telephone trackers, regional tracking coordinators, and the Retail Credit Bureau by grade levels. For example, the eleventh- and twelfth-grade follow-ups relied heavily on the regional coordinators and the Retail Credit Bureau. As the tracking effort progressed, however, staff concluded that the tracking would be better managed through a central operation conducted by in-house staff. The in-house staff conducted most of the tracking for the ninth- and tenth-grade follow-ups.

The multiple-approach tracking for the special nonrespondent samples was successful in locating and interviewing 86 percent of the former nonrespondents in the four 11-year follow-ups. The fact that Project Talent achieved a much higher relocation rate for the nonrespondent subsamples than for the general sample illustrates the increased effectiveness of tracking strategies that expend greater effort and resources to employ multiple approaches.

The case of the tenth-grade special sample of nonrespondents to the eleven-year follow-up questionnaire is instructive because Project Talent reports detailed information on the methods used to locate nonrespondents (Carrel, Potts, and Campbell 1975). Project Talent also reports information on the success and cost-effectiveness of using fifteen different information sources for tracking.

The design of the Project Talent study, like that of the National Longitudinal Surveys, is flawed for comparison purposes. Tracking methods were not randomly assigned to trackers or respondents, and controls were not introduced for prior methods employed or for order effects. The results must be viewed as suggestive but not definitive.

The results do support the importance of contacting parents and relatives of a panel member. Whether the approach was by community visit or telephone, information on primary family relations was the most successful way to relocate panel members efficiently and successfully. Project Talent put heavy reliance on telephone company information sources: directories and directory-assistance operators. About a fourth of the attempts at contact were successful. City directories, though not used as extensively as telephone directories, produced a 45 percent success rate. However, this method was expensive because telephone calls were placed to libraries and chambers of commerce for city directory information. Neighbors were difficult to contact, and that method was not used frequently.

Project Talent was fairly successful in utilizing the records of departments of motor vehicles, high schools, and colleges. Tracking through marriage records was also reasonably successful but very expensive. Birth and death records were seldom used and were never successful.

The National Longitudinal Surveys and the Project Talent follow-up data are based on a combination of community-visit and telephone approaches. The results suggest that tracking success depends on the approaches and information sources used. Nonetheless, the earlier caveats must be observed. Further, it is important to remember that these studies are based on two different approaches to national samples of restricted age distribution. Finally, the results will certainly vary with sample characteristics. Nonetheless, these studies provide the best cues to guide the use and anticipated success rates associated with selected information sources.

Efficient Use of Information Sources

Numerous information sources are available to trackers. The decision concerning which sources to pursue and in what order can be informed by guidelines or left to the discretion of the tracker. The former, if rigidly applied, precludes the flexibility needed to follow new leads as they occur. The latter may be a trial-and-error process and costly. Since it is desirable to reduce tracking costs and to maintain reasonable flexibility, it is prudent to establish a general search procedure that guides telephone and community-visit tracking. If multiple procedures are used, what information should the tracker pursue first? How should the rest of the search be structured? The answers to these questions are informed by understanding the hierarchy of information sources.

The ultimate source of information about the location of panel members is the respondent. However, reliance on respondents for address information presupposes a continuing interaction between respondents and the researcher. Procedures can be established to maintain contact with respondents over time, but these require effort and expense. Moreover, an appeal for help to gather information loses its immediacy and importance as time elapses. If the request is for a long-term continuing commitment, the cost for responding is prohibitively high for many respondents. Aside from financial compensation, a researcher lacks incentives that reduce the cost of responding.

If continuing contact over time with respondents is not possible, the researcher must reestablish contact. That can be like looking for the proverbial needle in a haystack. The problem is knowing where to look. One way to reduce the difficulty is to broaden the search to others who may know

where the respondent is. Unless there is a way to focus on particular information sources, this broadened search may be expensive.

Information sources can be ordered on two dimensions. The first is a
primary-secondary level distinction. *Primary-level relationships* are that
small number of people who know the respondent well. *Secondary-level
relationships* involve impersonal, segmented, and utilitarian contacts.

Four levels of primary-secondary relationships surround the respondent
and provide the social context for daily activities: family relationships,
social relationships, organizational affiliations, and public records (figure
4-1). Primary relationship information is usually the most accurate and
recent. As relationships become defined as secondary and social distance
increases, the information known about respondents is less accurate, less
current, less personal, and less detailed. It is limited to that required by
organizations of their memberships, or that required by public records.

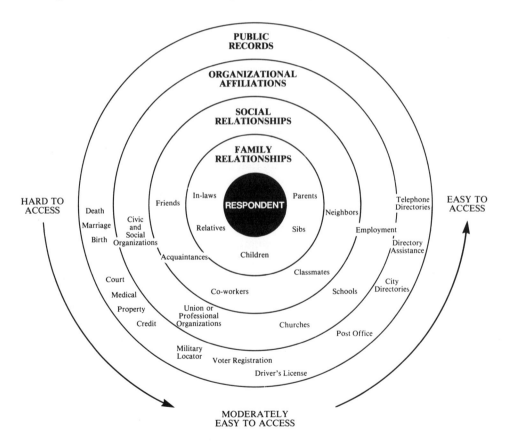

Figure 4-1. Levels and Accessibility of Information Sources

Figure 4-1 illustrates this ordering. The inner circles represent primary-level contacts. The outer circles are secondary-level information sources. The four levels characterize the quantity and quality of available information on respondents. The closer a tracker starts to primary relationships in accessing information, the higher is the probability that the information will be useful.

The second dimension by which information sources can be ordered occurs within the four levels. Sources vary in the difficulty there is to access the information. For example, parents are easier to identify than are in-laws or distant relatives (family relationships level). A respondent's neighbors are easier to identify than are friends who may live anywhere in a city (social relationships level). Employment plays a major role in everyday life, whereas civic and social organizations are often leisure-time activities (organizational affiliation level). Finally, some public records—for example, telephone directories and city directories—are easy to gain access to. Others—for example, birth certificates—are extremely difficult to gain access to, the cost is high, and the probability of success in locating the respondent from the information obtained is minimal (Willits, Crider, and Bealer 1969). Thus, the hierarchy of information sources can be ordered on two dimensions. As one moves between levels away from the respondent, the relationships become more secondary. And as one moves from left to right within levels, the ease with which a tracker can contact an information source increases.

Determining where a tracker should begin a search for mobile respondents depends on two considerations: the researcher's concerns regarding direct contact with respondents during tracking and the amount of respondent identification information available to the researcher. Sometimes it is not advisable to contact a respondent prior to data collection, and the search must begin at a different level to find people who know the respondent's current whereabouts. If, for example, the researcher has the name and address of family members, a tracker can initiate a search at the family relationships level. If the names and addresses of one or two friends are available, the search begins at the social relationships level, one level further removed from the respondent. If little personal information is available about the respondent, the search may necessarily begin in the outermost circle with public records. Tracking costs will be reduced and tracking success increased if researchers initiate the tracking effort with the most primary and the easiest to access information source.

Use of public records presents a special set of considerations. If a search of the easiest-to-access public records fails to locate the respondent, the search can be continued using those public records that are moderately difficult to gain access to. If the respondent still is not located, the search can turn to the hard-to-access public records, but this will be expensive and has little likelihood of success. We question the advisability of using hard-to-access public records and pursued these sources ourselves only in rare circumstances.

In summary, tracking is difficult not because respondents try to hide their whereabouts but when information is lacking or people are reluctant to help. The former problem is alleviated by beginning the search with sources closest to the respondent and easiest to gain access to. The latter problem is addressed by observing principles governing why people respond to requests for help.

Notes

1. Clarridge, Sheehy, and Hauser (1977) reported great difficulty in obtaining information from local schools because of strict interpretations of privacy regulations. They concluded that the high school is no longer a useful information source. We did not experience these difficulties in the Career Development Study. Apparently there is considerable variability by state, region, and perhaps period.

2. Microfiche copies are available from Bell and Howell Company, Microphoto Division, Old Mansfield Road, Wooster, Ohio 44691. The cost ranges from $175 for the ten largest metropolitan areas to $1,750 for areas of 25,000 or more population.

3. Antiquarians can sometimes locate copies of old telephone directories for a nominal fee.

4. The Directory Service Company in Boulder, Colorado, publishes rural directories for most counties in the upper central states. The Johnson Publishing Company in Loveland, Colorado, publishes city and community directories for selected areas throughout the United States.

5. It is seldom useful to contact neighbors other than those living in the two houses on either side of the respondent's former address and the residences directly across the street. Since most cities address houses with even numbers on one side of the street and odd numbers on the other side, it is usually easy to identify adjacent and opposite addresses.

6. An interlibrary loan request may be necessary. The request will be regarded more favorably if a letter specifies that this particular volume is critical to a program of research. This may prompt the local library to explore several available alternatives for providing access to the directories.

7. The high-use period is generally between 9:30 A.M. and 4:30 P.M. The operator staff is reduced during late evening hours, which increases demands on operators on duty.

8. Telephone companies report that directory-assistance operators achieve about 95 percent accuracy. Part of the error is due to the difficulty

in using paperbound or microfilm or microfiche systems where several books or fiche must be searched for a listing. AT&T estimates that by 1985, all Bell Operating Companies will convert to computer-based directory-assistance systems.

9. The addresses for the various military search services are as follows:

Army
Commander
U.S. Army Enlisted Records and Evaluation Center
Attention: PCRE-RF-L
Fort Benjamin Harrison, Indiana 46249

Air Force (Airmen)
World Wide Location Service
Airmen Branch
Military Personnel Records Center
Randolph Air Force Base, Texas 78148

Air Force (Officers)
World Wide Officers Location Service
Military Personnel Center
Randolph Air Force Base, Texas 78148

Navy
Commander
Naval Military Personnel Command
Department of the Navy
Washington, D.C. 20370

Marine Corps
Commandant
U.S. Marine Corps Headquarters
Code: JA
Washington, D.C. 20380

Coast Guard
Commandant
U.S. Coast Guard Headquarters
Washington, D.C. 20590

10. Temme (1975) reported that of 1,803 names published in news-papers, 23 percent were located and interviewed.

5

Tracking the Career Development Study Participants

We applied the Comprehensive Tracking Model to the Career Development Study at the Boys Town Center (1977-1981). In 1966 a team of researchers at Washington State University conducted a statewide study of the educational and occupational plans of Washington State high school students. A total of 6,729 juniors and seniors enrolled in twenty-five public high schools during the 1965-1966 school year completed questionnaires. The information included reports on high school experiences, school friendship patterns, attitudes toward school, study abilities, educational and occupational aspirations, and expectations.

As the questionnaires were distributed, the investigators asked students to complete a name-and-address form so that contact could be reestablished in the future. The investigators also selected and interviewed a random subsample (23 percent) of the original sample that provided a name-identification number record.

Thirteen years later we examined the educational and occupational achievements of these young people, who were about 30 years old during the restudy period. The Career Development Study required multidimensional life-history measures from each respondent. Volume I in the Entry into Careers Series (Otto, Call, and Spenner 1981) presented the sample design, the procedures for data collection, and the instrumentation used to gather the panel data. This chapter describes the development of the tracking strategy used to locate that panel.

The Study Parameters

Our tracking strategy reflected principles and procedures gleaned from previous studies and incorporated in the Comprehensive Tracking Model. Most studies reported that difficulties experienced in tracking were due to contingencies imposed on the research by the time 1 research design. By identifying and addressing these contingencies, we felt that serious problems contributing to sample attrition could be solved before they could surface during the tracking effort and jeopardize the outcomes of the study. Five areas for evaluation constitute the first step in designing a tracking strategy: contingencies that affect respondents' attitudes and behavior, resources, time, panel characteristics, and respondent characteristics.

Research Contingencies

We faced three contingencies. First, the panel members were former Washington high school students. Although dispersed across the state and nation, the respondents recognized and sometimes identified with the major Washington State universities. The current investigators were no longer located in Washington. This posed a problem of legitimizing the study in the minds of potential respondents.

We had access to mass-mailing services and a telephone-survey laboratory at our project offices in the Boys Town Center, Omaha, Nebraska. We arranged to conduct the study with the cooperation of the Social Research Center at Washington State University, an affiliation that eased the logistics of the long-range tracking endeavor. Also, identification with the university that sponsored the initial study provided a regional identification and legitimacy for the tracking effort.

Second, there is discussion and concern in the literature about changing public receptivity to social surveys (American Statistical Association 1974). The consensus suggests that the public is becoming less cooperative (Steeh 1981). Our response to this contingency was to avoid contact with the original respondent during the tracking phase wherever possible. We wanted to reduce the opportunity for a former respondent to refuse to participate on the basis of limited information about the study. To preclude a major cause of sample attrition, we focused on locating respondents through parents and other family members wherever possible.

Third, few people, whether panel members or their parents, remembered participating in the original study. Some respondents may continue to identify with their high schools, but most have left high school behind. Therefore, rather than stress identification with high schools, we approached the parent or respondent as a unique person who was important to the study. We personalized all communications and tried to foster attitudes of personal responsibility.

Resources

We had a modest but adequate budget for tracking respondents. We used facilities, recruited personnel, and applied financial resources such that we located 6,603 respondents at a cost of $8.62 per respondent.

Personnel. Tracking reports stress the need for well-trained personnel, but we did not have access to a pool of experienced trackers or to social science graduates and undergraduates.

The largest pool of potential trackers was women who lived close to the Center, had previous job experience, and were looking for part-time employment. None of them had tracking experience. We compensated for their lack of experience by providing orientation sessions, on-the-job training programs, close supervision, and a gradual introduction of different tracking procedures.

Facilities. We were well equipped to handle the tracking from the standpoint of facilities. We had access to a thirteen-booth telephone-survey room, a full-service library, a word-processing system, a PDP-11/70 minicomputer, a skilled computer programmer and software analyst, a print shop, and six IBM ink-jet document printers.

We did not have access to WATS lines. After thoroughly investigating WATS rates, we determined that existing rate structures were preferable. Our research offices were located in a state where charges were not made for directory assistance, and this was an advantage. Also, we produced personalized letters and prepared mailings at institutional rates of $171 per thousand, which was an attractive rate. In summary, we took full advantage of the facilities and services available to us at institutional rates.

Finances. Budgeting for tracking is problematic. Budgets are difficult to estimate because of the limited records of past experience and because there are few fixed costs. We based our estimates on seven expectations:

1. Fifty-five percent of the parents of former high school students would live in the same community fifteen years after their initial address was provided (Temme 1975).
2. Seventy-three percent of the former high school students would continue to live in the same state (Clarridge, Sheehy, and Hauser 1977).
3. Letters mailed to parents would produce addresses for 70 to 75 percent of the inquiries after four personalized mailings (Dillman et al. 1974).[1]
4. About 11 percent of the panel members not located through their parents could be located through the records and booklets of high school reunion committees (Temme 1975).[2]
5. An average of 3.6 phone calls would be needed to locate a panel member (Willits, Crider, and Bealer 1969).[3]
6. An average of seventeen minutes would be spent per telephone search for 60 percent of the cases (Clarridge, Sheehy, and Hauser 1977). The next 20 percent of responses would require an average of seventeen to twenty-seven minutes for each telephone search. From twenty-seven to fifty-three minutes per telephone search would be required for an additional 10 percent to raise the response rate to 90 percent.
7. The average phone call would take about five minutes to complete.[4]

On the basis of these assumptions, we estimated that it would cost $55,000 to locate 90 percent of our panel members, placing primary reliance on the mail approach, followed by telephone procedures.

Time

Twelve years had passed since the respondents were last contacted as juniors and seniors in high schools. In 1971, the original study team had attempted to obtain information on the students' educational attainments from the parents in a special interview subsample; however, the number of parents contacted was not sufficient to permit reliance on the six-year-old addresses. Thus, we tracked panel members on the basis of eleven- and twelve-year-old addresses.

One advantage of the timing of the follow-up study was the recency of ten-year class reunions. The reunion booklets provided addresses that were only one or two years old for 52 percent of the respondents.[5] Since fewer addresses were available from the reunion booklets than were potentially available from parents, we decided to contact the parents first and then use reunion addresses to contact respondents for whom parents were not contacted or failed to respond.

The study timetable and funding considerations limited the time we could allow for tracking. For budgetary reasons we decided to use mail as our primary approach and to follow with more expensive telephone procedures where necessary.[6] In order to shorten the time required to send multiple mailings first to parents and, if these were not successful, then to reunion addresses, we sequenced the mailings so that letters to parents that were returned as undeliverable established cases for the reunion-address mailing. This shortened the total time required by about four weeks. We set a goal of finding current addresses for 90 percent of our panel members in six months.

Panel Characteristics

The 1966 panel consisted of 6,729 students from twenty-five high schools in the state of Washington. Twelve years later the students were dispersed throughout the state, nation, and several foreign countries. Economies of scale dictated that we place primary reliance on the mail approach. Sample size required that we automate information collection and recording processes.

The 1966 data were well documented and included four types of information related to tracking:

1. The name-and-address cards of each student involved in the 1966 study;
2. Interview schedules that included the names and addresses of one-fourth of the parents of the respondents;
3. The names and mailing lists for a limited follow-up study conducted in 1971 that included about one-fourth of the panel members; and
4. The 1966 questionnaire and interview data.[7]

We faced two problems concerning the association of names of the original respondents with data cases. First, researchers seldom anticipate the need to retrieve additional information on respondents. Consequently, they collect little identifying information for tracking respondents in the future. The obvious piece of information is the participant's full name. In 1966 the respondents were asked to provide their name, mailing address, and high school. But the researchers did not specify that respondents should record full names, and many did not. Some provided initials, a nickname, or an abbreviated form of their name. Seldom was there a record of the parents' full names. Some respondents inverted first and last names. There was considerable difficulty deciphering the correct spelling of some names because respondents were not asked to print or to use a pen. Nevertheless we had the original name cards for reference where questions arose.[8]

A second problem was an absence of name cards for one small school (N = 79) serving several isolated rural communities. Project records indicated that for political reasons, the principal of the high school had decided not to return the name cards. We made a personal visit to explain the objectives of the follow-up study, and the current principal provided a list of the junior and senior students enrolled at the time of the original study. We linked students to their data records by calling or sending letters to ask them key questions about their earlier family histories and educational experiences.[9]

Incomplete or missing names for 75 percent of the parents complicated matters. We compensated for the lack of parents' names by using the 1966 marital-status variable to inform selection of an appropriate salutation and appending the respondent's recorded last name. For example, we addressed a letter to "Mr. and Mrs. Frederickson" if the data indicated that the parents were living together. Also, we added the respondent's name as addressee in order to provide the postal carrier with additional information. Thus, the envelope was addressed to "Mr. and Mrs. Frederickson or Rick Frederickson" at the address indicated by the respondent in 1966.[10]

Respondent Characteristics

The original sample design was a proportionate, stratified, random sample of Washington high schools (see Otto, Call, and Spenner 1981, chapter 5).

Juniors and seniors enrolled in the selected schools were asked to participate. The resulting sample included people from areas ranging from small, rural communities to large, metropolitan cities. Two percent of the sample was nonwhite, which was slightly less than the 4 percent expected on the basis of the state census (U.S. Department of Commerce 1970). The panel members came from families with slightly more advantaged socioeconomic origins than would be expected when compared with estimates for U.S. males. The most important characteristics of the panel were its age and sex composition. Since leaving high school, these respondents were geographically and socially mobile. Slightly under 50 percent were females. We expected that at least 80 to 90 percent of the females had married or otherwise changed their name (U.S. Department of Commerce 1979).

In summary, the tracking effort required procedures for dealing with a normal, mostly white population of mobile young adults.

The Multi-Method Approach

The assessment of the tracking parameters for our panel study resulted in four design requirements:

1. The time constraints of the funding period required that we complete the tracking quickly.
2. The amount of mobility and number of name changes required that our tracking procedures be flexible.
3. The large panel size and dispersion necessitated automating information collection and record keeping.
4. Financial considerations dictated that we automate components of the tracking effort

The first two considerations favored the telephone approach, the last two the mail approach. The telephone approach offered the quickest completion and least attrition, but available resources dictated the use of the less expensive mail approach.

We decided to use a multiple-approach strategy that offered the economy of automated mail and the flexibility of the telephone approach. The mobility of our population and the time that had elapsed since the last contact with respondents argued against use of the mail approach. But the mail approach could be used advantageously to contact parents, who were less mobile, and to pursue reunion addresses that were only a year or two old. Thus, we were able to apply an economical, automated mail approach to locate easy-to-find respondents and to focus the more expensive telephone approach on locating harder-to-find respondents.[11]

On the basis of previous research, we expected to receive 50 to 55 percent of current respondents' addresses from parents. If all respondents had addresses listed in their ten-year reunion booklets, we would have expected to add another 19 to 27 percent. But only half of our respondents were contacted by their reunion committees, and we expected response rates of 10 to 14 percent for letters mailed to reunion addresses. This expectation was consistent with Temme's (1975) experience.

In summary, we expected the mail approach to produce addresses for 60 to 69 percent of our panel. The telephone approach was held in reserve to locate panel members who were not reached through either mail procedure.

The Strategy

Other studies indicate that without an explicit, advance design detailing the tracking methodology, tracking becomes a high-risk enterprise and a burden of confusion and frustration.

The major contingency is the failure of a procedure to generate the desired result. By relying on multiple procedures, we reduced the impact of failure of any one technique. We planned backup techniques for ready implementation. This is not to say that a single tracking approach will not work. The Wisconsin Study, for example, was very successful with heavy reliance on telephone procedures, although the mail was used to contact respondents when a telephone number was not available. In large-scale panel studies, depending on a single method is too much of a risk and too costly.

We made two decisions in the interest of simplicity and diversity. First, we did not overlap our major tracking effort with data collection. On the positive side, this focused our efforts on finding current addresses. On the negative side, it increased the cost of tracking because some who were located moved before the telephone interview for data collection, which necessitated additional tracking.

A second potential problem was cost overruns in the event mail procedures were less successful than anticipated and heavy reliance would have to be placed on the telephone approach. Two mechanisms can be used to stay within budgets without jeopardizing data quality. One is to divide the panel into random subgroups and sequentially track subgroups until funds are expended. At that point tracking ceases and interviewing begins on the random subsample that was successfully tracked. The second is to locate addresses for the entire panel and then divide those cases into random subsamples so that interviewing can proceed until all funds are exhausted. Both methods maintain the integrity of the original panel because they randomly reduce the panel size. The second method merely compensates for cost overruns during tracking due to erroneous budgeting or faulty conclusions based on sampling error in the pilot study. Since we were reasonably confident about both our budget estimates and pretest results, we decided to use the latter procedure.

This decision established many organizational features of our tracking effort. We sequenced the major work loads so that no overlaps occurred. We spaced the mailings to parents and to respondents at their reunion addresses so that there were approximately ten days between each mailing wave (figure 5-1). Tracking by telephone was not begun until several letters were mailed to the reunion address, a procedure that enabled us to prepare and mail large mailing waves to parents and respondents before turning to telephone tracking.

The design schedule immediately filtered a case to the next tracking phase when a previous approach failed to locate an individual. If a letter to a 1966 address was undeliverable, we immediately checked the reunion file for a more current address. If there was no address, the case was assigned to telephone tracking. If a letter sent to a reunion address was undeliverable, that case was also immediately referred to telephone tracking.

As we completed the mail sequence of letters, we reassigned all cases where replies were not received from the parent or the respondent to telephone tracking. Our goal was to accelerate the process and reduce costs associated with the number of tracking personnel. Following this sequence, we were able to conduct the first two months of the tracking process with a staff of two full-time and three part-time people.[12] By the time we began telephone tracking, the mailing routines were sufficiently established that the project staff could turn their attention to telephone tracking.

We sequenced the telephone procedures to provide guidelines to trackers. The telephone approach used the respondent information as an initial reference point. From there we made a search of other information sources to update the earlier information. The limited amount of personal information initially available required that we reconstruct the respondent's family relationships, social relationships, and organizational affiliations in order to establish tracking leads. We followed a list of ten ordered procedures:

1. Consult 1966 city directories or telephone directories to ascertain the names of parents.
2. Consult current telephone and city directories to locate parents or respondents.
3. Search current and past telephone and city directories to identify people with the same last name as the respondent.
4. Contact high school class-reunion committee members for help in locating former classmates.

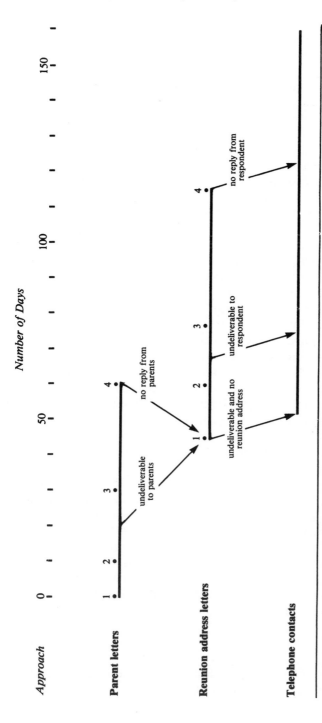

Figure 5-1. Proposed Schedule of Tracking Events in Career Development Study Tracking Strategy

Note: • denotes mailing date; 1, 2, 3, 4 represent the mailing wave.
Our goal was to locate 90 percent of the panel members in six months' time. The proposed schedule sequenced events in a five-month period so that time would be available for compensatory action.

5. Find current addresses for former neighbors (identified from 1966 city directories) or friends for additional information on missing respondents.[13]
6. Contact the former high school for information on the missing respondents.
7. Contact former employers of parents using employer information provided in 1966 city directories.
8. Search current telephone directories of major metropolitan areas in the states of Washington and Oregon for the name of parents or respondents; search surrounding community directories for all respondents who lived in a small Washington community in 1966.
9. Search public records or other official files by telephone or by letter.
10. Return name to the missing file for publication in local newspapers requesting community help in locating the respondent.[14]

The telephone procedures initiated the search among people closest to the respondent and then moved to public records that were feasible to search. The first procedure sought the names of close family members using the easiest-to-access public records (see figure 4-1). Once we established a name and telephone number for a parent, we phoned them. If the name for a parent could not be found, we made an effort to identify family members by using telephone listings for people with the same last name who may be related to the respondent. If the respondent still could not be located, we contacted classmates and the respondent's relatives, friends, and neighbors to inquire about the respondent. If these procedures failed, we contacted possible employers, churches, social and civic organizations, and high school personnel. In making these inquiries, the tracker tried to identify names and telephone numbers of people who knew the respondent or the family. Finally, we used city directories to identify parent's 1966 employer and contacted the listed employer for information and the names of former coworkers.

At this point, we exhausted all reasonable leads. The tracking effort had moved from people close to the respondent to organizations. As a final effort, we searched public records that were easy and moderately easy to access for information about the respondent. Finally, after all targeted tracking procedures failed, we used a shotgun approach during data collection in making a mass appeal to located respondents for information.

Our tracking strategy reflected an assessment of the Career Development Study parameters and consideration of the tracking principles incorporated in the Comprehensive Tracking Model.

The Mail Approach

One advantage of the mail approach is that the researcher communicates through both written words and visual cues. The addressee can scrutinize every component of a letter for information. The problem for the writer is identifying and including those components that convey the researcher's message without raising superfluous issues or concerns.

The researcher needs to ensure that respondents have sufficient information so that they will respond favorably. Respondents need six basic information items:

1. Who is writing?
2. How credible is the writer?
3. What is wanted?
4. How legitimate and important is the request?
5. Why should the respondent help?
6. How and when should the respondent help?

The initial impression of the importance of a request, the identity of the writer, and the credibility of the writer is conveyed by the outer envelope. Bulk-mail appearance conveys neither the impression that the message nor the recipient is special, and it is not likely to generate a favorable response.

We used a white, legal-sized envelope with the Washington State University return address. We printed the parent's name and address on the envelope. We used first-class postage in the form of a commemorative stamp.[15] We used the same type of envelope for subsequent mailings to respondents.[16] Letters to respondents differed only in that we stamped "address correction requested" on each envelope.

The mailings to parents consisted of a four-wave sequence of letters. We wrote each letter to communicate a specific message. The first letter to parents (figure 5-2) briefly presented the six points of information. We established who we were. We legitimized the study by using official university stationery and referring the parent to a university official if there were questions. We underscored the importance of the study by referring to the child's and parents' prior participation, by stressing the utility of the study, and by noting the usefulness of the study for resolving the feelings of inadequacy that parents have in advising their children on choosing a career (Elam 1978). We emphasized that in the earlier study the son or daughter had provided the parents' address as a location where he or she could be contacted at a later date. The request included a brief statement of the problem we faced in locating young people and our reliance on parents for help. We gave explicit instructions about what we wanted the parents to do. We enclosed a form that outlined the information we needed and requested an immediate reply (appendix A).

We communicated a considerable amount of information in the cover letter. We printed the letter with a smaller typeface to reduce the appearance of length and to increase the amount of white space on the page. People

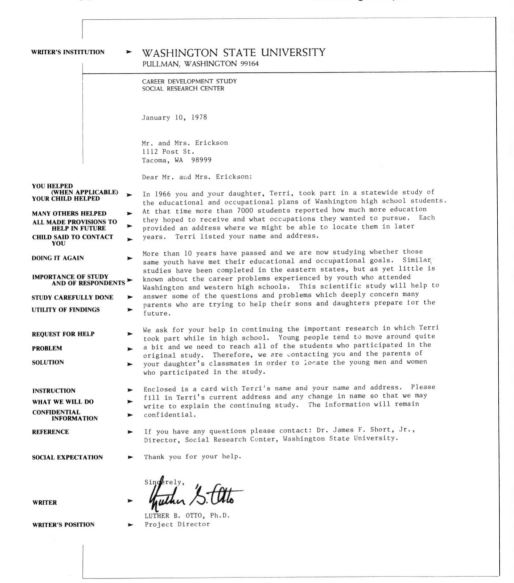

Figure 5-2. First Letter to All Parents

often skim letters for important points, so we divided the letter into six paragraphs. Each started with the most critical information we wanted to convey.

We personalized the letter with the name and sex of the son or daughter and used appropriate possessives and pronouns. The ink-jet printers automatically adjusted the line length to accommodate the variable text. The final product was a letter addressed to the individual parent.

We raised the psychological cost for nonresponse by a personal appeal to the parent and a reference to the panel member's willingness to be contacted at the parents' address in the future. We included a stamped, return envelope. This conveyed a trust that the parent would comply with our request.[17]

We reduced the psychological costs for helping by anticipating two major concerns. First, we minimized the time and effort the parent had to invest by providing a form for completion and a postage-paid, self-addressed, return envelope. Second, parents are usually protective of their children. We emphasized that we would explain the continuing study to their son or daughter. This assured the parent that the child would have a choice about continued participation in the study. We provided assurance that information given by the parent would remain confidential. Finally, rather than ask parents to write the child's address on the back of a postcard (which would have reduced postage but exposed the information to public view), we concealed the reply information by providing return envelopes, underscoring the confidential nature of our request.

We mailed a second letter to parents nine days after the first letter. We used the same outer envelope and return form. The purpose of the second mailing was to remind parents who had not responded that we needed a reply. Dillman (1978) suggested that the intent of the second letter is not to persuade the parents to respond but to jog the parents' memory and heighten the importance of responding. To accomplish this, we kept the letter very short and emphasized our need for assistance. The letter gave instructions on how to help (figure 5-3). In most multiple mailings the reminder is sent on a postcard, but we used a letter for emphasis. We enclosed a reply card and return envelope to maintain a close association between the attitude we tried to create and the behavior we expected from the respondent.

One of the realities of research is that what is needed is not always possible to achieve. The stamped, return envelope conveyed our message without superfluous stimuli, but the economics of return postage dictated that we use business reply envelopes on the second, third, and fourth mailings to parents. We printed the format of the business reply portion of the envelope as small as postal regulations permitted in order to reduce the prominence of the business reply layout. We positioned the return address so that the Career Development Study address was highlighted (appendix B).

The second letter was a reminder. The third letter encouraged response (figure 5-4); it was short but contained more information than the second. We reminded the parent of how much time had elapsed since our earlier contacts and that the child had helped us earlier. We emphasized the importance of their help. We provided instruction and underscored the need for an immediate reply. We closed the letter with a cordial reminder of our expectation. Again, we provided a form for completion and a return envelope.[18]

The fourth letter served dual purposes (figure 5-5). First, we presented additional information. Second, we sent it by certified mail with return

---

WASHINGTON STATE UNIVERSITY
PULLMAN, WASHINGTON 99164

CAREER DEVELOPMENT STUDY
SOCIAL RESEARCH CENTER

January 18, 1978

Mr. and Mrs. Jones
1111 Oakpark Drive
Seattle, WA 98999

Dear Mr. and Mrs. Jones:

REMINDER ➤ Last week we wrote to you and asked for Timothy's forwarding address so we can continue our study of Washington youth.

IF RETURNED, THANKS ➤ If you have already returned the card, we greatly appreciate your prompt assistance. If you have not returned it, simply
IF NOT RETURNED, INSTRUCTION ➤ complete the enclosed card by providing Timothy's current address and any name change. Please mail it today.

IMPORTANCE OF RESPONDENT ➤ It is very important that we reach all of the individuals who were part of this scientific study when they were younger.

Thank you very much.

Sincerely,

LUTHER B. OTTO, Ph.D.
Project Director

LBO/das

Figure 5-3. Second Letter to All Parents

receipt requested, which informed us to whom and where the letter was delivered.[19]

In this fourth letter, we encouraged attitudes favorable to response by noting the favorable responses of other parents and the concern parents typically have for helping their children. We reiterated the importance of

---

WASHINGTON STATE UNIVERSITY
PULLMAN, WASHINGTON 99164

CAREER DEVELOPMENT STUDY
SOCIAL RESEARCH CENTER

February 8, 1978

Mr. and Mrs. Adams
1113 Wall St.
Tacoma, WA 98999

Dear Mr. and Mrs. Adams:

REMINDER OF TIME THAT HAS TRANSPIRED ➤ About three weeks ago we wrote to you asking for the forwarding address of your son, John.

CHILD HELPED ➤ About 10 years ago, John was part of a long-term study of Washington youth. We now need to make contact with him in

IMPORTANCE OF CHILD'S RESPONSE ➤ order to update the information he provided to us while in high school. It is important that we be able to contact your

REQUEST FOR HELP ➤ son and we ask for your help in providing his forwarding address and any name change.

INSTRUCTION ➤ Please assist this important research by completing the enclosed form. Note John's current address and any name change and mail the card immediately. We anxiously await your reply.

SOCIAL EXPECTATION ➤ Thank you very much for your cooperation.

Cordially,

LUTHER B. OTTO, Ph.D.
Project Director

Figure 5-4. Third Letter to Parents

the son or daughter's assistance, an importance reinforced by the certified mailing. We reminded parents that the child had helped earlier and closed with a restatement of expectation for a reply. The difference between the fourth mailing to parents and the earlier letters was that it was less instructive and more direct about the issue of nonresponse.

WASHINGTON STATE UNIVERSITY
PULLMAN, WASHINGTON 99164

CAREER DEVELOPMENT STUDY
SOCIAL RESEARCH CENTER

March 10, 1978

Mr. and Mrs. Cooper
9999 Blondo St.
Tacoma, WA 99999

Dear Mr. and Mrs. Cooper:

REQUEST FOR HELP SENT ► Earlier we asked for your help in obtaining a current forwarding
EXPECTATIONS NOT MET ► address for your son, Charles. A reply to our letters has not
yet been received.

IMPORTANCE OF STUDY ► As you know, parents are very concerned about helping their
children choose the career which is right for them. We are
OTHER PARENTS HAVE HELPED ► greatly encouraged by the assistance that other parents have
given us. The success of this study depends heavily upon
Charles being able to let us know his experiences since high
RESPONDENT IS IMPORTANT ► school, insights that cannot be provided by his high school
classmates.

STUDY IS IMPORTANT ► It is important that we contact your son and we are sending this
letter by certified mail to insure delivery. Charles and his
RESPONDENT HELPED BEFORE ► classmates began this study with us when they were in high school.
Please complete and return the enclosed card. This will enable
LET HIM HELP AGAIN ► us to write to him to explain the continuing study.

SOCIAL EXPECTATION ► Thank you very much for your help.

Sincerely,

LUTHER B. OTTO, Ph.D.
Project Director

Figure 5-5. Fourth Letter to Parents (Certified Mail)

The reunion mailing consisted of letters addressed to panel members at the address in the reunion booklet. The three-wave sequence was similar to the first three parent letters in content, format, and schedule. We did not send a certified letter. We felt it might be counterproductive. The letters are presented in appendix C.

In summary, we adapted the mail approach to create attitudes in respondents favorable to our requests for assistance.

The Telephone Approach

Successful tracking by telephone depends on well-trained personnel, adequate facilities, and cooperative respondents. Because experienced trackers were not available, we compensated by scheduling a three-day training session for recruits. It covered the history of the study, an overview of what we wanted to accomplish, an introduction to tracking techniques, and a period of supervised practice calls. We assigned each tracker to find respondents from a particular school so that the tracker would become familiar with the high school, the community, and contacts in the community. We scheduled telephone tracking for Tuesday, Wednesday, and Thursday evenings and Saturday afternoons.[20]

The Project Talent and the Wisconsin Study experiences suggested that a well-equipped, centralized telephone facility assisted tracking efficiency for hard-to-locate cases. We provided the following materials and facilities:

1. A telephone-survey room equipped with thirteen telephones;
2. All current telephone directories for the state of Washington;
3. Current telephone directories for major cities in Oregon;
4. Telephone directories (Bell and Howell phonefiche) of the 246 major metropolitan areas in the country;
5. Polk directories for selected major cities in Washington;
6. 1966 or 1967 city directories for cities in which sample schools were located;
7. Maps of communities in Washington;
8. A zip-code directory and a telephone area-code manual; and
9. A computer terminal for access to current addresses of located respondents and the names of 1966 friends listed in the 25 percent subsample.

These provisions were adequate for conducting the nationwide search for our study participants. We stored the directories in a room adjacent to the telephone-survey room. This minimized noise and confusion in the telephone area and reduced interviewer fatigue by adding diversity to tracking routines.

We carefully planned telephone conversations to enlist cooperation. Unlike the mail approach, our telephone strategy relied on a short introduction and a request for help. We did not try to answer the six points of information discussed earlier. Rather, we got to the point immediately: "Can you help us?" The introduction was as follows:

Hello, is this the _____ residence? I'm _____ . We are working with Washington State University in conducting a follow-up study of former high school students. We are trying to obtain a current address for _____ who was a [junior/senior] at _____ High School in 1966. Can you help us?

The introduction identified who we were, why we were phoning, and what we wanted. The intent was to provide a minimal amount of information and to ask for a reply. This enabled the person to become involved in the conversation at an early point where either a sufficient amount of information had been given so that an address was provided, or the person could quickly identify specific concerns requiring additional information.

We anticipated the following three questions and answered them along these lines:

Question: Why do you want it [son or daughter's address]?

Response: In 1966 [son's or daughter's name] participated in a statewide study of seven thousand Washington high school students. We need to contact your [son/daughter] to provide information about the continuing study and to invite their participation.

Question: What is it [Career Development Study] about?

Response: In 1966 your [son/daughter] along with [his/her] classmates, provided information about [his/her] educational and occupational plans. Over ten years have passed, and we are now studying the experiences your [son/daughter] had during that time. We are interested in the accomplishments and problems young people face in trying to reach their goals.

Question: From where you are phoning?

Response: We are working with Washington State University on this project. I am phoning from Omaha, Nebraska, where we have a centralized location for contacting these young people who have moved all over the United States and the world.

We provided the replies to trackers as guidelines, encouraging them to modify the reply to suit their own interactional style and the situation. By providing a short, direct reply we hoped to decrease the time spent on the telephone and the amount of unneeded information provided to the respondent. We closed the conversation in this way:

> We really appreciate your help. Since we still have many students to locate, we will send _____ a letter in June explaining the study and inviting [his/her] continued participation. Thank you.

We used a different strategy to verify that a person was indeed a panel member. We started the conversation as follows:

> Hello, this is _____ ? I'm _____ and I'm working with Washington State University. We are trying to locate some of your former classmates from _____ High School. Do you remember [read off five names]?

This procedure focused on others and put the respondent in the role of a helper. In the course of clarifying the request for help, we verified the panel member's respondent status, and we often received information on other classmates.

In training sessions with trackers, we emphasized the importance of maintaining cordial relationships with the respondents. Trackers established positive attitudes about the continuing study by maintaining good tracking etiquette. This emphasis on cordiality undoubtedly improved the probability that a panel member would continue to cooperate during the data-collection phase of the study.

Record Management

We needed an efficient flow of information to accomplish our tracking within a six-month period. We had to move the names of missing panel members from one procedure to the next without delay and to record the information as we received it from respondents and other informants. We accomplished both by developing software for computerizing record keeping. This enabled us to determine the status and location of each person at any point in the tracking process. The amount of automation differed for the mail and telephone approaches.

The mail approach was extensively computerized. We generated mailing lists and letters from a master file that contained basic identifying information: respondent's identification number; 1966 name; 1966 address; indicators of parental marital status in 1966; respondent's sex; class in school in 1966; whether the person was part of the 1966 interview subsample; and the availability of a 1976 or 1977 reunion address. The file incorporated tracking codes designed to communicate the current tracking status of the panel member. We recorded each update together with the date when the change occurred.

The master file was the cornerstone of the automated process. We created two supplementary files to store reunion addresses and the most current available address for panel members who were located. We developed software to access the information to generate letters, to seek current or previous information, and to obtain daily summaries outlining the status of the tracking effort.

We automated record keeping most extensively for the mail approach. All mail returned to Washington State University was processed by a part-time assistant to establish the identification number printed on the return form (appendix A). The assistant pulled a computer card prepunched with the respondent's identification number. We developed a series of codes to describe the exact content of the returned envelope. For example, a letter returned with the current address and telephone number was coded "1." A return that contained only the address was coded "2." Codes also reported refusals and undeliverable letters. Based on the reply, the assistant coded and dated the prepunched identification cards, then mailed the punched cards on a daily basis to the project office. On receipt, we read the cards into the computer and changed the status of appropriate cases on the master file. The updated file provided a daily summary of results by school and date. We also used the update file to generate the list of identification numbers that we included in subsequent mailings.[21]

Telephone tracking does not accommodate the same level of automation as does the mail approach. For all of its efficiencies in other applications, automation is cumbersome for recording the amount of information gathered by trackers. Programs can be designed to record the information, but the process is inefficient unless each tracker has access to a terminal. Moreover, tracking involves the use of city directories. Logistically it is inefficient to record information from directories on a piece of paper and then transfer the information to computer files. For these reasons, we used a paper file system. Each respondent had a separate file that contained all information gathered about the respondent. We printed standardized reporting forms that trackers completed as they obtained information (appendix D). The process for updating the tracking status of respondents remained essentially the same. We entered updated address information daily into computer files.

The Pilot Test

Before we proceeded with the tracking strategy, we conducted a pilot test to establish the feasibility of the design procedures. We stratified the schools into five groups based on size and drew a random sample of twenty respondents from each of these groups ($N = 100$) for test purposes.

We generated letters on word-processing equipment and followed the preliminary design procedures. We located 75 percent of the subsample by mail.

We were pleased with the response rate but considered it to be high given the stratified nature of the sample, which favored smaller communities. After completing the mail procedures we attempted to contact the remaining subsample of panel members by telephone. The combined mail and telephone efforts proved successful in relocating 100 percent of the people in the pilot study. We established direct contact with 98 percent of the pilot subsample. Of the remaining two, one person was institutionalized and was not able to communicate. The second lived in New Zealand and did not reply.

The pilot study satisfactorily demonstrated the potential effectiveness of the Comprehensive Tracking Model applied to a subsample of Career Development Study participants. The exercise suggested minor adjustments to the tracking design and supported the feasibility of proceeding with the full-scale follow-up effort.

Notes

1. We assumed that the first two mailings consisting of a letter and a follow-up postcard would net a response rate of about 43 percent. A second reminder letter and a certified letter would increase the rate by an additional 17 and 12 percent, respectively.

2. We arrived at this figure by assuming that one-third of the addresses verified by the respondent had been obtained from reunion lists and two-thirds from the socioeconomic mailings and community canvasses.

3. The National Longitudinal Study of the High School Class of 1972 reported an average of two chargeable calls per respondent. About thirty minutes were expended for the hard-to-contact panel member (King and Thorne 1977). Rather than underestimate our costs, we used higher estimates reported by others.

4. The Rural Pennsylvania Panel Study reported calls taking two to three minutes each (Willits, Crider, and Bealer 1969). The Wisconsin Study reported thirteen minutes for exhausting leads by telephone and about three calls per case (Clarridge, Sheehy, and Hauser 1977). These figures average to 4.3 minutes per panel member. Project Talent estimated about five minutes per telephone contact (Carrel, Potts, and Campbell 1975). We followed the highest estimate.

5. Addresses were not listed for 43 percent. Five percent of our respondents' names did not appear in reunion booklets.

6. Our panel size and dispersion were large, and our offices were located some distance from Washington state. This ruled out the use of community

visits except in a few cases where reunion-committee people verified an address.

7. The original interview schedules and some of the original questionnaires were on file. Most of the original questionnaires had been destroyed after coding and keypunching. Evaluation of the data demonstrated that the coding and keypunching were reliable.

8. We found that 1966 and 1967 yearbooks from the high schools were useful in determining names.

9. We established the linkage by asking how students would have responded in 1966 to questions concerning father's and mother's education, father's occupation, number of children in the family, school grades, extracurricular activities, and future educational and occupational aspirations.

10. Address-name listings in 1967 city directories provided us with more adequate addresses and information where twelve-year-old directories were available. The trackers used the directories extensively. Where a 1967 directory was not available, trackers had difficulty developing leads.

11. Since the sample did not include a large number of difficult-to-locate people, there was little need for the personal contact and flexibility provided by the community-visit approach. Our use of reunion booklets, reunion-committee members, and telephone calls to communities gave us some of the benefits of community visits without the expense. Extensive use of the telephone can usually substitute for a community visit and does not involve the high costs of face-to-face contacts.

12. During preparation and mailing of the parent and reunion letters, our tracking staff consisted of a secretary, a research assistant, two part-time office helpers, and a part-time graduate assistant at Washington State University. Staff at the project office signed letters, affixed postage, verified mailing lists, updated computer records, and entered address information into the computer. The graduate assistant received the incoming mail at Washington State University and forwarded it to the project office in Omaha. Later, as the size of the mailing decreased, project staff prepared, assembled, and mailed the fourth-wave letters to parents and third-wave letters to respondents at reunion addresses.

13. In 1966, a 25 percent subsample identified junior and senior classmates who were best friends. We linked these names to participants in the study and recorded them by name and identification number in a computer file. Trackers used the file to request address information for friends during the tracking effort.

14. We never implemented this procedure. Rather, we included lists of missing respondents with the mail questionnaires sent to all respondents and asked for information on the whereabouts of missing classmates. Temme (1975) used newspaper advertisements to locate and interview 23 percent of the people whose names were listed in the advertisement.

15. The evidence on postage is inconclusive. Hensley (1974) reported that

different combinations of commemorative, regular, and metered postage did affect response rates. There may or may not be measureable differences between postage types, but commemorative editions catch the respondent's attention. We selected large and colorful stamps.

16. The first three mailing waves were scheduled nine to twenty days apart. Budget considerations favored printing, stuffing, sealing, and storing the entire sequence of four letters for each respondent. We then sorted the envelopes on the basis of nonresponse for follow-up mailings. We printed identification numbers on the envelope in the upper-right-hand corner. As we pulled letters for inclusion in a mailing, we affixed the large commemorative stamp over the number so that it concealed the identification number.

17. The impact of a stamped, return envelope on response rates is unknown but is probably not large. We used the stamped envelope to avoid eliciting attitudes about business that could arise if a business reply envelope was used. From a cost standpoint, business reply envelopes would have been less expensive. However, 45 percent of the letters were not deliverable and were returned. We retrieved the stamped, return envelopes and used them in subsequent mailings.

18. Apparently some people do not like to be viewed as late responders. Often people who responded late used the first card sent to them (we sequentially numbered each card) even though they had received other cards more recently. The ability of so many people to locate the earlier cards is anecdotal support for a benign-neglect explanation of nonresponse to surveys.

19. Even if the parent did not respond, we were able to ascertain the name of the person who received the mail. If the parents had moved, the new residents who had not bothered to notify the postal carrier of the incorrect delivery were requested to do so. In some small rural communities our earlier mail was held by the post office under the assumption that a new family was moving into the community. However, the certified letter forced the post office to return all such letters as undeliverable.

20. We decided to avoid Monday night television sports and Friday and Saturday evening activities when many young couples would not be home.

The importance of television sports to the general population should not be underestimated. One of our trackers telephoned a bar frequented by a panel member. The bartender informed her that there were three hundred screaming sports fans watching the championship basketball game and that she was crazy to think that the respondent would come to the phone. After several calls to other respondents with similar reactions, we halted tracking activities for the evening. We also had a parent abruptly hang up during the running of the Kentucky Derby.

Telephone calls placed by project staff during the pilot test indicated that a good portion of Friday and Saturday evening was spent talking to babysitters. The sitters could identify the respondent, but some were reluctant to provide information. Others did not know the desired information. Further, the telephone tracker lost the opportunity to ask the respondent about missing classmates.

21. The information cards containing the current name and address were later returned to the project offices. We entered the information on the cards into the computer file for access by telephone trackers and for use in subsequent mailings to respondents.

6

Tracking Outcomes in the Career Development Study

This chapter reports the results of our effort to locate the 6,729 panel members in the Career Development Study. The first part of the chapter reviews the tracking timetable and reports location rates for the approaches that we used. The second part reports tracking costs. Sections one and two demonstrate the success of our tracking strategy. An unanticipated delay in beginning our data collection required relocating some members of the sample. The third part of the chapter reports on that retracking effort. The chapter ends with an examination of the potential biases that were introduced by panel attrition related to tracking.

Timetable

The Career Development Study tracking effort began in December 1977. We mailed a letter to the principals and superintendents for the high schools in the sample explaining the continuing study and requesting the principal's assistance in identifying people who were responsible for ten-year class reunions. A week later we telephoned each principal to obtain the information requested in the letter.[1]

On January 10, 1978, we initiated the mail sequence to parents for the total sample. Table 6-1 summarizes the dates and the sequence of letters sent to parents and respondents in each mailing wave. We conducted the mail procedures over a ten-week period. During that time we processed 19,393 letters. The last mailing occurred on March 27, 1978.

Location Rates

Our goal was to locate 90 percent of the panel members within six months. We reached the goal five months after we began the tracking effort. We regarded the 90 percent success goal as the lowest acceptable level of achievement and continued some tracking through completion of data collection. Eventually we located current addresses for 98.1 percent ($N = 6,603$) of the panel members.

Table 6-2 reports the final disposition for the cases sought. About 75 percent of the cases classified as institutionalized, deceased, or family located

Table 6-1
Mailing Dates, Type of Letter, and Number of Letters Posted

Date	Letter Type	Number Posted[a]
January 10, 1978	Parental wave 1[b]	6,726
January 18, 1978	Parental wave 2[c]	6,726
February 8, 1978	Parental wave 3	1,813
February 22, 1978	Reunion wave 1[d]	1,486
March 3, 1978	Reunion wave 2[e]	1,486
March 10, 1978	Parental wave 4[f]	442
March 22, 1978	Reunion wave 3	552
March 27, 1978	Reunion wave 1[g]	162
Total		19,393

[a]The panel consisted of 6,729 people; however names were not available for one small school. We identified and tracked these people by telephone procedures. In addition, about 76 names and addresses were available for people who did not have data present from the 1966 data collection. The original investigators excluded some questionnaires because they were incomplete or invalid. We tracked these people, used them as a pretest sample for the telephone interview, and included them in our estimates of the number of letters posted. Thus, the number of letters posted does not necessarily correspond in some of the tables that follow.

[b]Personalized letter sent to all parents.

[c]Reminder letter sent to all parents.

[d]Personalized letter sent to respondents using addresses from 1976 or 1977 high-school reunion booklets.

[e]Reminder letter sent to all wave 1 reunion letter recipients.

[f]Certified letter sent to parents who had not responded.

[g]Special mailing to respondents from two high schools for which we had difficulty obtaining reunion booklets.

were males. Of the 97 people whose family could not be located, 56 percent were females. Seventy-six percent of respondents located and available for an interview ($N = 4,897$) continued to reside in Washington. Most who moved out of state did not migrate far. Sixteen percent took residence in the Pacific and Rocky Mountain states, notably California, Oregon, Alaska, and Idaho. The remainder scattered across the nation (7 percent) and the world (1 percent).[2] We located panel members in every state except Rhode Island.

We expected that most of our respondents would continue to live in the state of Washington, but we were surprised at the number living close to their 1966 residence. Twenty-three percent ($N = 1,559$) lived an average distance of one mile from their 1966 address.[3] Forty-five percent of the panel lived within twenty-five miles of their 1966 home. A slightly higher percentage of males than females (48 percent versus 43 percent) lived within twenty-five miles of their 1966 residence.

Other researchers have noted the tendency for students to remain in the state where they attended high school (Willits, Crider, and Bealer 1980; Clarridge, Sheehy, and Hauser 1977). Since many young people continue to

Table 6-2
Final Location Status for the 6,729 Career Development Study Panel Members

Final Disposition	Number	Percentage
Current address found		
Available for interview	6,457	96.0
Institutionalized	31	.4
Deceased[a]	115	1.7
Subtotal	6,603	(98.1)
Current address not found		
Family located[b]	29	.4
Family not located	97	1.5
Subtotal	126	(1.9)
Total	6,729	100.0%

[a]Most deaths due to automobile accidents.

[b]In most instances, we located parents and close relatives. Relatives referred us to parents who refused to provide addresses. It appeared that many of these people were hiding from creditors, law officials, and ex-spouses.

live in-state, an understanding of in-state mobility patterns is useful information for trackers. The Career Development tracking effort provides a case study that suggests post-high school, within-state mobility patterns that may apply more generally.

Mobility Patterns

The Cascade Mountains divide Washington State into two distinct areas (figure 6-1). East of the mountains, the state has an agricultural economy. Spokane, the second most populous city in the state, has the largest metropolitan area. Four other cities of 15,000 to 50,000 population bound the western and southern boundaries of the east side of the state. In contrast, western Washington contains many densely populated areas with a diversified economic base, including aerospace, shipbuilding, finance, refining, fishing, timber, shipping, and recreation industries. The vast majority of the population and industry of the state is concentrated in the Puget Sound area around Seattle.

Given the geographic, labor market, and population differences, it is not surprising that students from the east were less likely to remain in the same community (22 percent remained in the east, 27 percent in the west) and on the same side of the state (35 percent remained in the east, 46 percent in the west).[4] About 17 percent of the former high school students from the east side moved to the west side of the state within twelve years after leaving

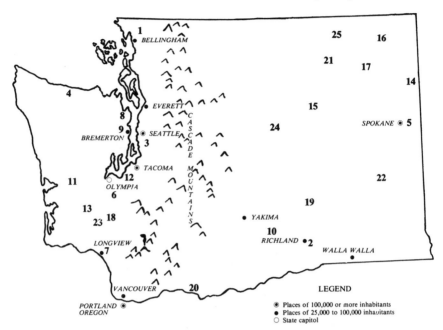

Note: The school number represents location and school size relative to other schools in the sample. The largest school is identified by "1." People living around school 20 have difficulty traveling to the major eastern Washington cities due to poor roads but can travel with ease on the interstate highway to Portland. Therefore, we considered school 20 to be a western Washington high school.

Figure 6-1. Geographic Location of the Twenty-Five Washington High Schools Included in the Career Development Study

high school. Three percent of the western Washington high school students moved east over the same period. Males were more likely to live close to their 1966 residence. Females were more likely to remain on the same side of the state.

Former high school students from rural areas were relatively easy to track because their parents seldom moved. If a parent could not be found, the closeness of large population centers appeared to make a difference in determining how far the former rural student would move from the high school community. Students attending rural high schools on the east side of the state and who continued to live in-state were less likely to remain in the community (23 percent versus 33 percent) but more likely to stay on the same side of the state (55 percent versus 42 percent) compared to their urban counterparts. However, there was very little difference in the mobility patterns of western Washington rural and urban students who remained in-state.

The differences between eastern and western students were illustrated further by the distances students moved from their 1966 residences. About 50 percent of western urban, western rural, and eastern urban students lived within twenty-five miles of home twelve years later. Only 28 percent of the eastern rural students remained within twenty-five miles of their home town.

We interpret these findings as follows. The best place to look for urban and rural students who lived in or near densely populated areas is the communities or neighborhoods in close proximity to their high school residence. If a search in the local area fails to locate a respondent who lived in an isolated rural area, a search should be made of the larger cities close to the rural area, followed by a search of the major metropolitan areas in the state.

Mobility patterns are evident for young people who remained in the state, but patterns are less evident for those who moved out of the state. Few personal characteristics distinguish those who remained from those who left Washington. Females migrated out as much as did males. Both the 1966 and the 1967 high school graduating classes had about 24 percent of their classmates living outside the state.

To explore the incidence of selective migration, we examined the impact of three general types of variables associated with out-state mobility (Willits, Crider, and Bealer 1980). The first set of variables was indicators of family background. We reasoned that more-advantaged family circumstances would favorably affect the respondent's opportunity to leave the community. The measures of family background included father's level of occupational status (Duncan SEI), father's and mother's years of education, parental marital status (scored 0 or 1 with 1 = intact), number of siblings, gender (scored 1 or 2 with 2 = female), and continued parental residence in same community (scored 0 or 1 with 1 = letter still deliverable to 1966 address).[5]

High achievements in high school and aspirations to continue formal education may attract students to institutions of higher education in other states. We included the respondent's self-reported grade point average in 1966 for the last semester in school (0 to 4.0 scale) and the respondent's expectations for years of completed education to measure this possibility.[6]

Finally, actual personal achievements and other life course contingencies may induce or require the student to leave the state. Limited access to high status jobs, the pursuit of higher education, marriage, and military service are common contingencies. We used the socioeconomic status of the respondent's current or most recent job (Duncan SEI), years of formal schooling completed, number of marriages, number of children, and military service (scored 0 or 1 with 1 = served in the military) as measures of achievement and contingencies. While not exhaustive, these fourteen indicators provided us with a first look at the effects of some major variables typically associated with social mobility and geographic mobility. For purposes of this analysis out-state mobility was defined as a dichotomous variable (scored 0 or 1 with 1 = current out-state residence).[7]

We used these fourteen indicators to predict out-state mobility and the distance the respondent had moved from 1966 residence. Father's years of education, respondent's military service, current job status, grade-point average, and expected years of education had small significant positive impacts on out-state mobility and distance moved.[8] Parents' continued residence in the 1966 community had a small significant negative impact on out-state mobility. Together these variables explained only 3 percent of the variance in mobility and distance moved. Thus, family background, aspirations, and achievement variables do not differentiate those who moved out of the state from those who remained, nor do they predict how far a student will move.

Schools with 100 to 150 students in the junior and senior classes had the highest average percentage of students that left the state: 37 percent. The average for other schools was 26 percent. About half of all panel members who moved from the state moved to major metropolitan areas.

We cannot explain either the distance respondents moved or their tendency to move out of state on the basis of social and demographic variables associated with social mobility. However, panel members who live near state lines and move to an adjacent state are likely to be found in the major metropolitan areas of that adjacent state. Those who move to nonadjacent states are equally likely to be found in metropolitan or nonmetropolitan areas.

Response Rates for Tracking Approaches

Our tracking strategy involved a planned sequence of approaches. It started with a series of four letters mailed to parents at their 1966 addresses, followed by a three-letter series mailed to respondents at their 1976 or 1977 addresses, and concluded with telephone calls. The later two approaches were coordinated. We refer to these approaches as the parent letter, the reunion letter, and the telephone search.[9]

Figure 6-2 plots the search for a respondent through the three-stage process beginning with the parent letters. We began the telephone search only after we tried the parent letter and reunion letter approaches. Thus, the results are not comparative evaluations of three separate tracking approaches but the descriptive outcomes of a flow of events.

Parent Letters

We first mailed a sequence of up to four letters to parents at the addresses provided by respondents in 1966. The parent letter was delivered to 54 percent

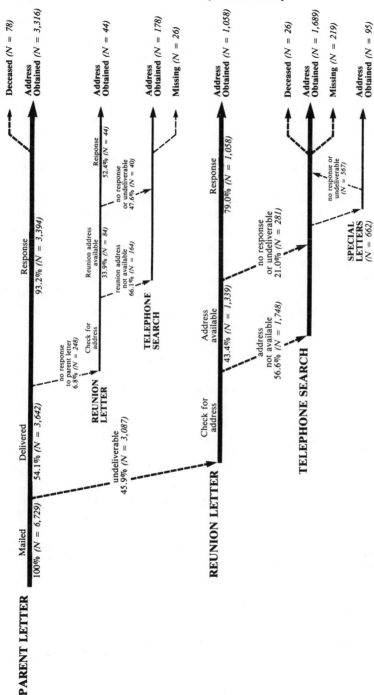

Figure 6-2. Sequence of Approaches and Location Rates through November 1978

of the parents (figure 6-2) from whom we received current addresses for 50 percent ($N = 3,394$) of our panel members. Considering only the letters delivered, we obtained a 93 percent response rate from parents.

Examination of the mailings and response dates indicates that 52 percent ($N = 1,907$) of the letters delivered prompted a response within fourteen days of the mailing. The follow-up reminder letter sent to all parent addresses caused a surge in the daily returns. Seventy-seven percent ($N = 2,791$) of parents who received the letters replied prior to the third letter. The first three letters produced responses to 88 percent ($N = 3,215$) of the delivered letters. The certified letters produced another 179 responses.

The response rate to the mail approach was higher than we expected. Our rules of thumb proved useful for planning purposes. One percent fewer letters were delivered than we expected, and we exceeded the expected level of response by 18 percent. We mailed the certified letter to 442 parents. It served its function well: over 40 percent of the parents to whom this letter was mailed responded with a current address for their child.

Not only did the number of responses exceed our estimates, but the responses were returned earlier than expected. We received 49 percent of the total responses within ten days of the first mailing. Ten days later, it was 73 percent. At that point, the return rate began to slow. Thirty days after initiation of the mailing procedure, we had received 82 percent of the responses. After another thirty days, we had 95 percent of the responses. We received almost all replies within eighty days of the first mailing.

Table 6-3 reports the percentage of letters delivered by schools represented in our panel. It is evident that most rural parents of respondents did not relocate during the twelve-year period or, if they did, the postal carrier knew where to forward the letter. About half of the letters were delivered in large urban areas. However, all but a few letters mailed to one city were returned to us as undeliverable. We later learned that the city had renamed the streets several years after the initial data collection. Another small school that had a very low delivery rate served mostly military families.

In summary, the parent-letter phase of our tracking strategy proceeded as planned and exceeded our anticipated response rates.

Reunion Letters

In the second sequence of our tracking strategy, we mailed letters to addresses obtained from ten-year class-reunion booklets (figure 6-2). Our analysis is based on returns for the eleven largest high schools in the sample.[10] The reunion lists covered 83 percent ($N = 5,613$) of the total panel.

Table 6-3
Letters Delivered to Parents in 1978, by High School Attended

School	Number of 1966 Juniors and Seniors	Percentage of Parent Letters Delivered
1	901	53
2	828	60
3	827	53
4	650	46
5	531	60
6	495	24[a]
7	466	58
8	328	57
9	314	75
10	212	50
11	192	69
12	155	16[b]
13	118	60
14	102	75
15	101	67
16	93	51[c]
17	71	5[d]
18	71	79
19	61	51[c]
20	49	84
21	39	85
22	34	97
23	38	71
24	27	78
25	26	69

[a]City had renamed most city streets. Almost all mail was returned as undeliverable as addressed.
[b]School served military families stationed at Fort Lewis Army Base.
[c]At the time of the survey, major dam construction took place close to these towns.
[d]Name cards not returned in 1966. We sent a few letters to parents after their names were established.

Reunion booklet addresses covered 52 percent (N = 3,493) of our panel members, or 62 percent of the people listed in a reunion booklet. Five percent of the panel members were not listed as class members.[11]

Reunion booklets contain biases that our data expose. First, reunion committees for classes having more than four hundred class members located about 46 percent of their classmates. The average for reunion committees that searched for 325 or fewer former classmates was higher—about 75 percent. Apparently class size greatly magnifies the difficulty that reunion committees experience in locating their classmates.[12] The percentage of classmates that reunion committees located varied from a low of 27 percent for a school with over eight hundred study participants to over 82 percent for a school with about three hundred panel members. Committees from smaller schools located higher percentages of their classmates.

A common notion is that reunion committees locate more classmates in the local area than in areas farther away. Table 6-4 shows that reunion committees do contact more classmates living in the same community; however, committees are also successful in contacting about half of all other classmates irrespective of the distance they have moved. Our letters to parents achieved higher response rates, but the distributions of percentages found for each area of the country are remarkably similar.

Reunion committees find about 52 percent of their classmates, while letters mailed to parents are delivered to about 55 percent of the parents. Are the students located by reunion committees similar to those found by mailing a letter to parents? Table 6-5 demonstrates that mailing a letter to the parents' 1966 address and the reunion committee's efforts to locate former classmates both produce about 40 percent of the respondents the other effort misses. The 40 percent located by the letter to parents may represent the failure of the reunion committee to contact parents living in the same residence ten years later, or it may represent nonresponse by parents to the reunion committee's request. The 40 percent located by the reunion committees may represent the reunion committees' knowledge and access to community information sources to obtain a current address.

Another common perception is that reunion committees have more success in contacting students who had higher visibility: students who come from higher status families, had higher scholastic achievements, dated more often, were active in high-school activities, and generally had higher attainments in their later life. To examine this argument, we added an indicator of dating frequency, the number of extracurricular activities in which the student participated, and a measure of the distance respondents

Table 6-4
Percentage Located by Reunion or Parent Source, by 1979 Place of Residence

	Place of Residence in 1979						
	Same Community	Same Side of State	Other Side of State	Western States	All Other States	Foreign	Not Found or Deceased
Reunion address[a]							
Not available	38	48	46	53	53	49	89
Available	62	52	54	47	47	51	11
Parent letter							
Not delivered	40	51	44	52	56	58	100
Delivered	60	49	56	48	44	42	0
N	1,656	2,748	493	1,056	426	76	274

[a]Address taken from reunion booklets for the eleven largest high schools represented in the Career Development Study.

Table 6-5
Reunion Address Availability, by Delivery Status of Parent Letter

| | Parent Letter | |
	Not Delivered	Delivered
Address in 1976 or 1977 reunion booklets		
Not available[a]	57%	41%
Available	43	59
N	3,087	3,642

[a]Includes 322 panel members whose names were not listed in reunion booklets.

had moved from their 1966 residence to the fourteen variables we used earlier. These variables were regressed on a binary reunion address variable (1 = an address available).

The respondent's current job status, gender, and years of expected education, as well as parents' marital status, had small positive impacts on the availability of a reunion address. The distance the respondent moved and the number of siblings had small negative effects. Parents living in the community contributed moderately to availability of an address (beta = 0.13). However, all of the variables taken together explained only 4 percent of the variance in reunion address availability.

If there are respondent characteristics that determine the availability of reunion addresses, they are not the usual indicators of family background, aspirations, achievements, attainments, or social visibility. The major biases in reunion address lists are in coverage. First, it is difficult to obtain reunion lists or booklets for small, rural communities. Second, only about half of the students are located. Third, reunion committees report addresses more often for females than for males.

Taking these and the biases of the parent letters into account, there do not appear to be compelling coverage advantages or disadvantages to using either ten-year reunion addresses or twelve-year-old mailing addresses in tracking. These findings are based on data from a state that has a history of in-migration. There may be differences in states experiencing out-migration.

One consideration in the decision to use parent or reunion addresses is the advisability of reducing the number of contacts with the respondent to avoid uninformed refusals. This suggests that it may be advisable to use the reunion address as a backup procedure to the parent letter.

The parent letter obtained addresses for 3,394 respondents, leaving 3,335 people to find by other means. Of these, 43 percent (N = 1,423) had a reunion address. A total of 1,102 people responded to the three mailings, for a response rate of about 77 percent to the reunion letters. There were fewer reunion addresses for respondents whose families refused to provide an address and a smaller percentage of those respondents replied than in the larger mailing (figure 6-2). Given findings about differences in individual characteristics, it appears that the parents who refused to respond dislike responding to any requests for help, whether from researchers or from people in the community.

We received quick responses to reunion letters. After twenty days, responses were received from 57 percent ($N = 627$) of those who would eventually respond. After thirty days, the response rose to 80 percent. Thereafter the rate of response slowed dramatically, although a few letters were returned up to 184 days after the initial mailing. The pattern of responses was almost identical to the distribution of responses received from parents; however, over 93 percent of the parents responded, but only 77 percent of the reunion letters confirmed a current address. This difference in response rates suggests that it may be advisable to use the parent contact prior to a reunion letter.

In summary, the response to the reunion letters supported our expectations for this portion of the tracking strategy. The mailing to reunion addresses raised the number of respondents located by 16 percent. At this point we had established addresses for 67 percent ($N = 4,496$) of our panel members using the relatively inexpensive automated mail approaches. We turned our attention to locating the more difficult cases.

Telephone Search

In April 1978 we initiated the telephone follow-up procedures. After three days of training, nine part-time trackers began by searching for current addresses for panel members whose parent letters were returned as undeliverable by the post office. About two weeks later, the trackers also began to pursue those cases for which the reunion letters were returned as undeliverable. After the trackers had experience with tracking the easier cases, we assigned them to cases where parents refused to provide addresses and to respondents who had not replied to the reunion letter.

The telephone search sought addresses for 2,233 panel members. We located a current address for 89 percent ($N = 1,988$). We placed 8,277 long-distance calls at a cost of $6,543.55, or an average cost of $2.93 per person sought and $3.29 per person located. The average long-distance call cost $0.79 and lasted three minutes. We made an average of 4.1 calls per respondent located.

The length, time placed, and destination of long-distance calls are the major determinants of direct-dial, long-distance charges. We placed most calls during weekday evening hours and on Saturdays. Eighty-seven percent of the long-distance calls were made to locations in Washington. The length of the calls ranged from one to seventy-one minutes. Seventy-seven percent of the calls lasted less than three minutes, 62 percent less than two minutes, and 38 percent lasted one minute or less. About 6 percent of the calls lasted more than seven minutes. We placed most of the more lengthy telephone calls to community contacts or reunion-committee members concerning a large number of people.

A telephone tracker sometimes received an address for a panel member or a panel member's friends or parents who could not be reached by telephone. We sent special letters to pursue these leads (see figure 6-2). The letters were not highly successful, but they were necessary in situations where a contact in a community could not be established to check a lead. Reunion people helped us considerably by pursuing hard-to-find leads locally.

The procedures were reasonably successful in the initial reduction of attrition. Only six people refused to continue participation in the study based on the information we presented by telephone. Our success in reducing attrition by reducing refusals later carried over into the data-collection effort where only 3 percent ($N = 191$) of the people contacted refused to participate.

The refusals during data collection vary by tracking approach (table 6-6). People whom we contacted by mail were more likely to cooperate during data collection than were people we tracked by telephone. These data do not necessarily mean that a particular tracking approach causes attrition during data collection; however, the outcome does illustrate that the more intensive tracking effort locates people who are difficult to find or may have a greater tendency to refuse to participate.

Tracking Costs

We summarize our expenditures for relocating participants in table 6-7. We allocated expenditures between the major methods and averaged across

Table 6-6
Telephone Interview Status, by Type of Tracking Approach

| | Tracking Approach | | | |
	Parent Letters	Parent Letter Refusals	Reunion Letter	Telephone Search
Telephone interview status				
Incomplete	2.0%	12.8%	2.0%	4.9%
Complete[a]	98.0	87.2	98.0	95.1
N	3,186	187	1,024	1,666

[a]Complete includes thirty interviews that we completed but declared invalid due to interviewer error, computer malfunctions during interviewing, and other irregularities.

Table 6-7

Summary of Tracking Expenditures, January-November 1978

	Mail	*Telephone*	*Total*
Postage (stamps, international reply coupons, return postage charges)	$ 4,878.97	$ 0	$ 4,878.97
Materials (office supplies, stationery, envelopes, printed record forms)	3,011.30	365.81	3,377.11
Printing (two sets of four-wave personalized correspondence)	5,558.26	0	5,558.26
Telephone lab charges (charges for twelve telephone hook-ups and monthly charges)	0	1,260.00	1,260.00
Telephone charges (primarily direct-dial, evening, and Saturday rates)	0	6,543.55	6,543.55
Staff salaries and benefits (fractional time for project director, secretary, and research assistant)	9,999.12	6,573.36	16,572.48
Personnel (part-time for clerical tasks, class-reunion committee assistance)	2,447.77	0	2,447.77
Telephone trackers (part-time)	0	7,133.00	7,133.00
Search materials (phone fiche, telephone and city directories)	0	3,109.96	3,109.96
Computing charges (programmer for software development, billings)	2,600.00	1,655.00	4,255.00
Washington State University, Social Research Center Charges (computing, indirect cost, miscellaneous)	430.48	0	430.48
Travel and per diem (field visit to two schools)	0	715.56	715.56
Totals	$28,925.90	$27,356.24	$56,282.14
Average cost per person located[a]	$6.15	$14.97	$8.62

[a]Averages based on 6,805 names (panel members and pretest respondents). Mail procedures accounted for 4,702 people and telephone procedures located 1,828 people. By November 1978 the total located was 6,530. Eventually we located 6,603 respondents.

respondents located. Finally, we totaled direct costs, but did not adjust to include institutional indirect costs.[13]

Nearly all cost figures are based on actual expenditures for which receipts and time-and-effort statements exist. Where estimates are included, the figures represent upper estimates. Where supplies were ordered, we report the total costs, including unused materials earmarked for data-collection procedures. Where in-house charge-back procedures for services did not exist—for example, computing costs, software development, acquisition of library materials, and reference materials for tracking—we calculated the costs on the basis of standard rates charged elsewhere.

Our records indicate an average relocation cost of $8.62 per respondent to locate 96 percent of the panel.[14] Two considerations must be observed in evaluating this cost. First, direct comparisons with earlier studies must be adjusted for cost increases in wage scales, postage, materials, telephone tariffs, and service rates. Second, these figures should not be generalized to research settings that have their own configuration of resources and cost structures that must be taken into account in developing an effective and efficient tracking design. Nonetheless, our experience indicates that relocation of respondents in long-term and large-scale panel studies can be cost-effective.

Retracking

A number of people move or change telephone numbers between the time they are located and interviewed. One advantage of collecting the data shortly after or during tracking is that the number is minimized.[15] The longer the period between tracking and data collection, the more mobility occurs and the probability of panel attrition increases. People are more difficult to locate a second time.

We were forced to postpone the initiation of data collection. The decision to proceed with data collection was not made until December 1978.

Prior to data collection, we initiated procedures for verifying the accuracy of telephone numbers on file. We found that 66 percent of the listings remained the same, 30 percent changed, and listings could not be found for 4 percent of the panel members previously located. About a fourth of the changes in listings were due to a telephone company decision to reassign numbers for the outskirts of Seattle. We obtained new listings for most of these respondents from directory assistance, but a number of people requested that their new numbers be unpublished.

We obtained telephone numbers for all but 2 percent of the panel members for whom we received an address by mail. The reply card asked the parents to provide their own and their child's current address. Cards sent to respondents asked them to correct their address and provide their parents' address. Most complied with the request and provided both. Respondents were much more reluctant to provide their parents' address and telephone number when contacted by telephone. About 6 percent of the respondents whom we located during the telephone search could not be quickly relocated. The highest loss rate, however, occurred for respondents whose parents refused to respond to the parent letter. About 13 percent of these people were not found during the verification process. Their parents refused to provide address information even though in some instances we could document that their child had provided us a previous address. Had respondents been asked earlier to provide the names of two people who would always know their whereabouts, it would have been much easier to reestablish contact with these people.

Most of the retrack effort occurred during December 1978. Trackers placed 3,521 long-distance calls to locate new listings for about one thousand people.[16] The average long-distance call lasted 2.4 minutes and cost $0.62. Eighty-six percent of the calls were less than three minutes long. Just under 90 percent were placed into the state of Washington.

We began data collection in March 1979. We had to retrack 746 people during data collection. Reliable time and cost estimates are not available for this retracking effort.

At the conclusion of the interview by telephone during data collection, we verified the respondent's current address with the respondent. Later we mailed questionnaires that included a request for information about the respondent for future follow-ups. We also asked for help in locating people whom we were not able to contact (appendix E). The latter procedure helped find the hard-to-locate.

Panel Biases

One of the consequences of panel attrition is the possible differential impact of lost cases on substantive estimates. We explored how much bias we might have introduced had we not pursued tracking respondents as extensively as we did.

We split the panel into four groups that represent the tracking events illustrated in figure 6-2. We present the means and standard deviations for selected 1966 questionnaire data and 1979 telephone interview data in table 6-8. The variables represent family background and achievement indicators commonly used in several areas of research. We conducted tests for mean and variance differences among the four groups.[17]

We note several mean differences for the people we tracked by telephone, but we did not anticipate the general lack of substantive differences in mean values between the four tracking processes. With the exception of parental marital status, there are not significant mean differences in the family background variables between the four tracking groups. However, all three high school achievement and aspiration variables demonstrate significant mean differences between the tracking groups. Of the attainment variables, only the respondent's current job status differs significantly across groups. In each of these cases, the mail approach locates people with higher status aspirations or achievements than those located by telephone. Stopping the tracking effort at this point would have led to an upward bias in mean estimates of these socioeconomic variables.

Table 6-8
Means and Standard Deviations of Selected Variables, by Tracking Approach

	Parent Letter		Parent Refusal		Reunion Letter		Telephone Search		Total		Level of Statistical Significance	
	X̄	SD	X̄	SD	X̄	SD	X̄	SD	X̄	SD	X̄	Variance
1979 Data[a]												
Military service	0.23	0.42	0.29	0.46	0.21	0.41	0.25	0.44	0.24	0.42	n.s.	n.s.
Number of marriages	1.00	0.56	1.12	0.68	1.06	0.53	1.08	0.62	1.04	0.57	n.s.	.001
Number of children	1.46	1.12	1.70	1.12	1.48	1.08	1.52	1.16	1.49	1.12	n.s.	n.s.
Years of formal education	14.51	2.09	13.56	1.77	14.22	2.06	13.96	1.98	14.29	2.06	n.s.	n.s.
Current job status	48.25	22.76	41.33	21.81	48.50	21.64	45.98	22.45	47.48	22.50	.01	n.s.
1966 Data												
Gender	1.48	0.50	1.44	0.50	1.55	0.50	1.49	0.50	1.49	0.50	n.s.	n.s.
Father's job status	44.10	26.02	40.15	27.96	44.23	24.79	43.65	26.07	43.87	25.91	n.s.	n.s.
Father's years of education	12.55	2.98	12.06	2.95	12.39	2.87	12.35	3.02	12.45	2.98	n.s.	n.s.
Mother's years of education	12.52	2.30	11.86	2.16	12.33	2.22	12.22	2.29	12.37	2.29	n.s.	n.s.
Number of siblings	2.67	1.80	2.94	1.88	2.65	1.68	2.84	1.89	2.73	1.81	n.s.	n.s.
Parental marital status	0.90	0.30	0.88	0.33	0.82	0.38	0.78	0.42	0.85	0.36	.001	.001
High-school grade point average	2.67	0.79	2.28	0.75	2.64	0.76	2.49	0.82	2.60	0.80	.001	n.s.
Educational aspirations	15.38	1.86	14.67	1.91	15.28	1.90	15.10	1.95	15.26	1.90	.05	n.s.
Educational expectations	15.03	1.75	14.28	1.80	14.92	1.80	14.70	1.83	14.89	1.79	.01	n.s.
N	3,390		239		1,057		1,917		6,603			

[a]Includes only respondents who completed 1979 interview.

Only two variables demonstrate significant differences in variance across tracking groups: respondent's number of marriages and parental marital status. Estimates of variance in these two variables are more restricted for the mail approaches. Both sample mean and variance differences reflect respondents whose parents have greater marital stability if located by the mail approaches. If our original data had included the names of brothers and sisters or their mother's married name and address, we might have been able to circumvent tracking problems associated with parental marital status.

The two mail approaches contacted a cross-section of the original sample. Since there were relatively few differences in family background variables, mail approaches that locate more than half the parents in a large sample appear to provide a subsample of respondents whose social background closely approximates values for the larger sample. We might have anticipated these findings from the manner in which the mail approaches cut across all mobility patterns, whether in- or out-state.

These findings do not diminish the problem of attrition in panel studies, however. We found significant mean differences for several respondent behaviors and attitudes. Since the respondent, not the parent, is the subject of the study, significant bias could occur if researchers do not utilize tracking approaches that locate hard-to-find respondents. In addition, the data cover limited variables, do not speak to covariance patterns, and generalize only to the population we studied.

A second consideration favoring extensive tracking is the study objectives. Our research objectives required life-history data. These have numerous permutations, and a large number of valid cases is required to capture this diversity for analysis. Failure to locate the hard-to-find respondents may restrict the number and bias the sampling of life-history permutations in the data.

In summary, this chapter presented the results of our application of the Comprehensive Tracking Model. The procedures successfully tracked 98.1 percent of our panel members in a manner that reduced attrition during data collection. The data lend support to the Comprehensive Tracking Model. Nonetheless, considerable work needs to be done in examining the utility of various components of the model. The development and application of the model is an attempt to establish tracking methods and procedures that reduce attrition and keep tracking costs to a minimum.

Notes

1. We reviewed the details of the study and asked for the names of the class-reunion committees. The advanced information on the study established

principals as community opinion leaders and created a climate of school cooperation and local participation in the Career Development Study.

2. Of the seventy-six people who lived outside the United States, nineteen lived in Canada (all but one lived in Vancouver, B.C.), twenty-eight in foreign countries (largely in Europe), and twenty-nine were with the U.S. armed forces overseas.

3. We computed distances as the number of miles traveled between the geographic centers of zip codes. When respondent's 1966 and 1979 zip codes were identical, we used the average distance across the geographic area covered by the zip code. In most instances, this average distance was about one mile in urban areas. In rural areas, the actual distance was greater; however, this is not reflected in the distance estimate because there was greater use of post office boxes in rural areas.

4. The definition of community is restricted to mean identical zip codes for the respondent in 1966 and 1979. In large urban areas, *same community* refers to a small urban neighborhood. In rural areas, the geographic area becomes much larger.

5. We converted father's and mother's education levels from a grade to a year metric by assigning the following conversions: completed eighth grade or less = 8 years; ninth through eleventh grades = 10 years; twelfth grade = 12 years; one through three years of college = 14 years; four years of college = 16 years; and more than four years of college = 18 years. The effect is to bias the year indicator slightly downward inasmuch as we do not know how many years parents spent in school beyond four years of college. Since we assigned the last code to several hundred parents, it is likely that many had more than the two additional years of college education assigned them by this coding scheme.

6. We coded respondent's expected years of formal education by making the following conversion: quit high school = 11 years; to just graduate from high school = 12 years; to attend business, vocational, or technical school = 13 years; to attend a junior college or a nursing school = 14 years; to attend a college or university = 15 years; to graduate from a college or university = 16 years; and to complete graduate work = 18 years.

7. The variation in the dependent variable is restricted. Only 24 percent of the panel members moved out of state.

8. By *small* we mean a standardized regression coefficient of a magnitude between .05 and .10.

9. We refer to the 248 parents who did not respond as the *parent refusals*. We consider this group separately because they arrived at the reunion letter search in a different way than the rest of the panel members.

10. We encountered considerable difficulty locating reunion lists for high schools in rural communities. In most instances, reunion booklets were not available. If a name list was printed for the reunion, few people retained

the list. Usually we had to locate the person who chaired the reunion to get a list. As a result, we obtained the available reunion lists for rural areas during the early part of telephone tracking.

11. The omission of these names was largely due to high school dropouts, residence changes before graduation, and reunion committee error.

12. The size of the metropolitan area in which the high school was located does not appear to make a difference. Some of the high schools with two hundred to three hundred in a graduating class were located in metropolitan areas similar in size to the largest high schools in our sample.

13. The base for calculating indirect charges varies by institution. We included all charges except estimates for physical facilities and utilities.

14. About 1 percent of the sample was located after we halted the record keeping on tracking expenses.

15. We did not overlap the major tracking effort and data collection in the Career Development Study. To maintain the importance of tracking, we planned data collection to follow shortly after tracking was completed.

16. Directory-assistance operators provided most new listings if the respondent moved within the same city and continued to list a telephone number. We did not keep records of the exact number of new listings operators provided, but our trackers estimate that directory assistance provided about half of the new listings.

17. For technical reasons we conducted statistical tests of significance on a 13 percent random sample of all respondents ($N = 874$).

7 Epilogue

A necessary condition for the success of panel research is reestablishing contact with study members. Over three decades ago, Lazarsfeld (1948) observed that the panel technique was a slow and expensive research operation. He emphasized that it would require money, time, and arduous work to develop the technique into a useful tool. Twenty years later, Eckland (1968) noted that researchers had to rely on their own experience or the personally communicated experiences of others to devise a tracking design. Eckland's review failed to find a single comparative study of tracking techniques, though it did provide insights into successful tracking procedures used in several large panel studies. Another thirteen years have now passed. During this period we find only one modest comparison of the relative effectiveness of tracking techniques (Willits, Crider, and Bealer 1969). In addition, a small number of articles and monographs have appeared outlining the successes of several large-scale tracking efforts (Freedman, Thornton, and Camburn 1980; Clarridge, Sheehy, and Hauser 1977; Temme 1975).

The Comprehensive Tracking Model takes the tracking enterprise a step beyond its development in previous research. The model revolves around a logic for why people respond. This logic informs the overall tracking design and guides its day-to-day implementation. Applications of the model occur in the context of parameters: investigator resources, time, panel characteristics, and respondent characteristics. The model also proposes principles and refinements that instruct the development and implementation of a tracking strategy. Our application of the model in the Career Development Study demonstrates its potential power and success. The model proved efficient and cost-effective.

The Comprehensive Tracking Model has applications to other populations, panel sizes, and time parameters beyond that recorded in chapter 5. Yet the model does not offer a set of definitive propositions grounded in systematic empirical applications. It is a heuristic tool based on our own experience and assessments of the advantages and disadvantages of the various tracking approaches and information sources reported by others. We have been cautious to avoid the appearance of presenting empirically derived parameters and refer to our estimates as rules of thumb. The translation of these rules of thumb into general propositions requires empirical research not yet accomplished. We see three areas that require further research and more rigorous information gathering.

First, the efficacy of the mail, telephone, and community-visit approaches in situations with differing mixtures of parameter values (resources, time, panel characteristics, and respondent characteristics) is an open question. Comparative assessments of the three approaches are lacking, as are assessments of the efficacy of combinations of mail, telephone, and community-visit approaches. We developed a preliminary assessment of the tracking approaches based on the work of Willits, Crider, and Bealer (1969) and the accumulated experiences of others. From this account we developed our most important hypothesis: that a sequenced combination of mail and telephone approaches is the most efficient and cost-effective for locating panel members in typical applications of the Comprehensive Tracking Model. Community visits have demonstrated success in locating hard-to-contact respondents, but this approach is prohibitively expensive in large tracking efforts.

Second, the relative effectiveness of tracking information sources is largely unknown. Rigorous research comparing information sources does not exist. In chapter 4 we reviewed the major information sources and organized them in terms of their primary-secondary level relationship to the respondent and their ease of access to trackers. We offered two hypotheses drawn from our own experience and subject to independent verification. First, it is best to initiate the tracking process at the most primary-level information source. Second, the tracking process should pursue information sources, whether primary or secondary, in order of ease of accessibility. We offer the hypotheses for research verification.

Third, we counsel that researchers regularly obtain identifying information from respondents during the initial data collection. We suggest this practice even if the probability of a subsequent follow-up is not strong. There is little research evidence for what personal information is most important. Yet common sense, our experiences, and those of others suggest some guidelines. The student information form recently used by the High School and Beyond Project offers a good example (National Opinion Research Center 1980). The investigators gathered the name, address, and telephone number of the student and his or her parents; the student's birthdate; the names of three high school friends who were seniors; the names, addresses, and telephone numbers of two persons who would always know where to contact the respondent; and the respondent's driver's license number, social security number, and nicknames if applicable. In many research studies, this extensive information request may not be possible, and the choice of which information to request is left to the investigator.

Our application of the Comprehensive Tracking Model was to a large, heterogeneous sample, twelve years out of high school. We offer our informed speculation on the model's application to other parameter situations. We note that the central tenets of the model—a logic for why people

respond, a reasoned tracking strategy, and implementation informed by organizational principles and refinements—are postulated to hold across
tracking situations for samples of several hundred or a few thousand
respondents.

Perhaps the most basic variation from one study to another is in panel
size. As panel size increases, the importance of automation and the necessity
of using multiple-tracking approaches also increases. Departures from this
norm will be less cost-effective, will require more time to locate a target
number of respondents, or will locate fewer respondents if we adjust for
time and resource expenditure. As panel size decreases, say from thousands
to several hundred, automation is not as important, particularly if labor
costs are low. Often reduced panel size is correlated with less panel and
respondent heterogeneity, which at reduced levels permit a tracking design
to place greater reliance on one or another tracking approach.

Federal Regulations and Ethical Issues

Tracking involves using sources of information to locate a person's
whereabouts. Tracking may be affected by federal legislation, reviews by
human subjects review committees, and school board policies regarding access to school records. The issue of access to information is more salient today than ever before in the history of scientific research.

The principal piece of federal legislation that affects tracking is the
Family Educational Rights and Privacy Act of 1974, commonly referred to
as the Buckley Amendment (Public Law 93-380). The intent of the Buckley
Amendment was straightforward: to provide parents greater access to their
children's school records and to protect the confidentiality of personal information in school records. The act did make provision for the release of
directory information (for example, student name, address, date and place
of birth, and field of study) without written consent from parents or the student. Local educational institutions have considerable latitude to define the
content of directory information. Moreover, parents or eligible students
have a right to withhold release of all directory information. Enforcement
of the act and related legislation is embodied in a substantial set of federal
regulations (Office of the Federal Register 1979).

We offer several observations with respect to the regulatory legislation
and its enforcement. Most important, we found a substantial range of interpretations over what constitutes directory information, when the regulations apply, and to whom exceptions were granted. Most educational institutions were willing to provide what is reasonably defined as directory information under current guidelines. For this reasons, the legislation and
regulations had little net effect on our tracking operation.

Compliance with legislation and regulations aside, we feel that there are also ethical considerations concerning how researchers deal with respondents. How a researcher treats a respondent, defines the respondent in conversations with others, respects the privacy of the respondent, and guards the information confided to the researcher—these are not only issues of research practice but are also matters of professional ethics. We followed several operating procedures that we believe served the respondents' best interests and our own research purposes. The first was that we observed courtesy in our relationship with respondents. We avoided late-evening calls, interruptions at work, and calls during meals and other inconvenient hours. If a respondent was busy, we offered to call back at a more convenient time or to accept a collect return telephone call. We attempted to reimburse respondents who did not have telephones for their inconvenience and expense in using the telephone during the data-collection phase.

Second, we offered as much information about the larger study as the respondent requested, whether in writing or by telephone, even if it required a telephone call from the principal investigators. A number of such calls were made. We took the position that the respondent had a legitimate right to know the complete answer to any reasonable question about the study seeking his or her participation.

Third, if a friend or relative of the sample member suggested that the person would not want to be located or to participate, we continued to track the panel member and directly offered the opportunity to continue in the study. The large majority of such respondents graciously gave their consent. If a sample member was hesitant during the tracking or data-collection phases, we offered to have the project director call to answer any questions and to explain the larger study. A number of such calls were also made. At this point, if the panel member chose not to participate, we honored that preference and considered the case a refusal.

Perhaps the strongest support that we can marshal in favor of this approach is the record of cooperation and goodwill that we received from the Career Development Study participants. We found very little, if any, evidence that sample members found the tracking or extensive data-collection effort an invasion of their privacy. Of the 6,729 people we tried to track, fewer than ten wrote and expressed concern about intruding on their private lives.

Prior to data collection, we provided each respondent with a brochure that explained the study in detail. It informed panel members of the type of questions we would ask and gave an address they could use to obtain further information. Of the names forwarded for telephone interviewing ($N = 6,095$), only 191 (3 percent of the total sample) refused to participate. Many respondents voluntarily prepared for the telephone interview; they reconstructed their life histories in advance of the interview by checking on schooling dates or compiling their own job calendars.

Later in the data collection, we sought access to respondents' high school transcripts and standardized test scores. Following federal regulations, we requested written permission from the respondents to obtain those records. Of respondents who returned a mail questionnaire ($N = 4,936$), 97 percent also returned a signed permission form.

Finally, at the end of the mail questionnaire we provided space for optional, open-ended comments. We asked people about the major problems they had encountered since leaving high school and what might be done in high school to help young people prepare for the future. We expected that a modest to small number of people would respond with a sentence or two. Indeed, the items were intended as "cool out" questions to ease the respondent out of the questionnaire in a favorable way. But we were wrong: over 4,200 people responded to one or both questions. Thousands of respondents provided substantial hand-written responses containing multiple paragraphs. Hundreds went further: some wrote in small print in the margins; others attached an extra sheet; some typed a composed response. None of this extra effort was requested.

Many respondents thanked us for the opportunity to do the interviews and commented that it was a unique opportunity to reflect on major life events since leaving high school. A great many respondents requested information on the results of the study. About a year after data collection, we mailed a brief report that described some general findings to each respondent. We still receive occasional letters expressing continued interest in the study.

In summary, the respondents' cooperation was excellent. Given courtesy, provision of full information, and forthright explanation of the larger benefits of the study, the vast majority of respondents did not feel that there was an intrusion on their privacy or an imposition on their time during either the tracking or data collection phases of the study.

Ironically, the ethics of privacy became a larger issue for us as record keepers than as information gatherers. Many respondents, including some high school reunion committees, inquired about the whereabouts of their former classmates. Some parents who did not know the location of their sons or daughters requested that information. In many cases, we surmise, the respondent preferred being "lost" because of serious personal problems or a desire to avoid family disputes. Honoring our guarantee of absolute confidentiality, in no case did we provide any personal information, including address and telephone number, to a third party, including parents. If the request seemed reasonable, we offered to forward a letter to the respondent mailed to us by the third party. We always left the decision to the respondent whether to reestablish contact with the third party, and we did so in writing. Our position on this sensitive issue was accepted and respected by all inquirers.

Federal legislation and regulations appeared to be quite ominous at the onset of the study, but in retrospect we observe that they were not a major detrimental factor in the tracking effort and data collection. Our sense is that they serve the public good without building impassable barriers to responsible research. If there was a problem, it was the wide discrepancy in how educational institutions defined directory information for former students.

Respondents expressed curiosity rather than concern about how we were able to find them after so many years. The tracking procedures appeared to foster a perception that we respected our respondents and were genuinely interested in their well-being.

The Importance of Tracking

Attrition in large-scale panel studies can be reduced to a minimum by following the Comprehensive Tracking Model. Expectations for attrition rates over 25 percent in large panel studies are no longer reasonable or acceptable. Most panel members can be located and interviewed in an efficient and cost-effective manner.

Improvements in tracking strategies may have benefits far beyond research applications. Several recent events underscore the policy significance of a well-grounded tracking theory and methodology. For example, in 1957 an estimated 2,250 U.S. military personnel took part in a nuclear test, nicknamed "Smoky." Operation Smoky participants now appear to have abnormally high rates of leukemia. Similarly, as many as 250,000 other military personnel may have been exposed to excessive radiation in a number of nuclear tests during the 1950s. Although there is a substantial amount of information available about these people, on at least one occasion the army has acknowledged its inability to relocate the former Smoky participants (*Washington Post*, January 26, 1978; February 15, 1978). As a result, early warning signals are not monitored, and precautionary health procedures are not being followed.

More recently, evidence is mounting that a substantial number of people have been exposed to hazardous substances. For example, it is estimated that about 4.5 million workers in U.S. naval shipyards received potentially hazardous exposure to asbestos. Millions of people who came in contact with the workers also may have been exposed (*Washington Post*, April 27, 1978). To date the government has engaged in passive tracking through the media, physicians, and labor unions. In Senate hearings held in 1977, the National Institute of Occupational Safety and Health estimated that it would cost up to $40 million to find and notify the estimated 21 million people who had been exposed to all types of hazardous substances. Our cost data suggest that the $1.90 per person estimated may have seriously underestimated the real cost. Yet the tracking costs, whatever they may be, must be measured against the personal and financial costs of catastrophic illnesses. We suggest that a large portion of these populations could be located and referred for medical evaluation at an acceptable cost if appropriate tracking theories and methods were followed.

Future tracking efforts will require more planning and advance preparation to achieve the efficiencies offered by the Comprehensive Tracking Model. In particular, we urge researchers to gather key information from respondents during first-wave studies. This strategy avoids the inefficiencies of reconstructing primary group contacts and locating information sources at subsequent data-collection points, and it does so at minimal cost. The Comprehensive Tracking Model offers an efficient and cost-effective strategy that enhances the viability of panel studies in scientific research and may have social benefits yet to be realized.

Bibliography

Alwin, Duane F. "Making Errors in Surveys." *Sociological Methods & Research* 6 (1977):131-150.

American Institute of Public Opinion. *Religion in America: 1977-78.* Gallup Opinion Index Report. No. 145. Princeton, N.J.: American Institute of Public Opinion, 1978.

American Statistical Association. "Report to the ASA Conference on Surveys of Human Populations." *American Statistician* 28 (1974):30-34.

Barnes, Hilda N. "Finding and Interviewing the Hard-to-Locate: The DMI Experience." In *Evaluating the Impact of Manpower Programs*, edited by Michael E. Borus, pp. 145-154. Lexington, Mass.: Lexington Books, D.C. Heath, 1972.

Bright, Margaret. "A Follow-Up Study of the Commission on Chronic Illness Morbidity Survey in Baltimore: I. Tracing a Large Population Sample over Time." *Journal of Chronic Disabilities* 20 (1967):707-716.

Campbell, A. Angus; and Katona, George. "The Sample Survey: A Technique for Social-Science Research." In *Research Methods in the Behavioral Sciences*, edited by Leon Festinger and Daniel Katz, pp. 15-55. New York: Holt, Rinehart and Winston, 1953.

Carrel, Kathleen S.; Potts, Clifford A.; and Campbell, Emily A. *Project TALENT's Nonrespondent Follow-Up Survey: The 10th Grade Special Sample*. Palo Alto, Calif.: American Institutes for Research, 1975.

Clarridge, Brian R.; Sheehy, Linda L.; and Hauser, Taissa S. "Tracing Members of a Panel: A 17-Year Follow-Up." In *Sociological Methodology 1978*, edited by Karl F. Schuessler, pp. 185-203. San Francisco: Jossey-Bass, 1977.

Coleman, James S. *The Adolescent Society: The Social Life of the Teenager and its Impact on Education*. New York: Free Press, 1961.

Coombs, Lolagene; and Freedman, Ronald. "Use of Telephone Interviews in a Longitudinal Fertility Study." *Public Opinion Quarterly* 28 (1964):112-117.

Crider, Donald M.; and Willits, Fern K. "Respondent Retrieval Bias in a Longitudinal Survey." *Sociology and Social Research* 58 (1973):56-65.

Dillman, Don A. *Mail and Telephone Surveys: The Total Design Method*. New York: Wiley, 1978.

Dillman, Don A.; Christenson, James A.; Carpenter, Edwin H.; and Brooks, Ralph M. "Increasing Mail Questionnaire Response: A Four State Comparison." *American Sociological Review* 39 (1974):744-756.

Eckland, Bruce K. "Retrieving Mobile Cases in Longitudinal Surveys." *Public Opinion Quarterly* 32 (1968):51-64.

Elam, Stanley M., ed. *A Decade of Gallup Polls of Attitudes Toward Education 1969-1978*. Bloomington, Ind.: Phi Delta Kappa, 1978.

Fetters, William B. *A Capsule Description of High School Seniors Base-Year Survey. National Longitudinal Study of the High School Class of 1972*. Department of Health, Education and Welfare. Washington, D.C.: U.S. Government Printing Office, 1974.

Fondelier, Sharon E. "Keeping Track of Respondents in Longitudinal Studies." Paper presented at AMA/Census Conference, October 1976.

Freedman, Deborah A.; Thornton, Arland; and Camburn, Donald. "Maintaining Response Rates in Longitudinal Studies." *Sociological Methods & Research* 9 (1980):87-98.

Freedman, Jonathan L.; and Fraser, Scott C. "Compliance Without Pressure: The Foot-in-the-Door Technique." In *Beyond the Laboratory: Field Research in Social Psychology*, edited by Leonard Bickman and Thomas Henchy, pp. 71-77. New York: McGraw-Hill, 1972.

Gallup Opinion Index. *Religion in America: 1977-78*. Princeton, N.J.: American Institute of Public Opinion, No. 145.

Glasser, Gerald J.; and Metzger, Gale D. "National Estimates of Nonlisted Telephone Households and Their Characteristics." *Journal of Marketing Research* 12 (1975):359-361.

Groves, Robert M.; and Kahn, Robert L. *Surveys by Telephone: A National Comparison with Personal Interviews*. New York: Academic Press, 1979.

Heberlein, Thomas A.; and Black, J. Stanley. "Attitudinal Specificity and the Prediction of Behavior in a Field Setting." *Journal of Personality and Social Psychology* 33 (1976):474-479.

Hensley, Wayne E. "Increasing Response Rate by Choice of Postage Stamps." *Public Opinion Quarterly* 38 (1974):280-283.

Homans, Celia. "Finding the Hard-to-Locate: The NORC Experience." In *Evaluating the Impact of Manpower Programs*, edited by Michael E. Borus, pp. 155-164. Lexington, Mass.: Lexington Books, D.C. Heath, 1972.

Kanuk, Leslie; and Berenson, Conrad. "Mail Surveys and Response Rates: A Literature Review." *Journal of Marketing Research* 12 (1975):440-453.

King, Donald A. *National Longitudinal Study Data Collection Activities for the Fourth Follow-up*. Technical Report prepared for the National Center for Education Statistics, U.S. Department of Health, Education and Welfare. May 1981.

King, Donald A.; and Thorne, Nancy R. *National Longitudinal Study Data Collection Activities for the Third Follow-up (July 1976 through June 1977)*. Final Report prepared for the National Center for Education Statistics, U.S. Department of Health, Education and Welfare. September 1977.

Kish, Leslie. *Survey Sampling*. New York: Wiley, 1965.

Lazarsfeld, Paul F. "The Use of Panels in Social Research." *Proceedings of the American Philosophical Society* 42 (1948):405-410.

Lazarsfeld, Paul F.; and Fiske, Marjorie. "The 'Panel' as a New Tool for Measuring Opinion." *Public Opinion Quarterly* 3 (1938):596-612.

Lewis, Morgan V. "Finding the Hard-to-Locate: A Review of Best Practices." In *Evaluating the Impact of Manpower Programs*, edited by Michael E. Borus, pp. 165-173. Lexington, Mass.: Lexington Books, D.C. Heath, 1972.

McAllister, Ronald J.; Butler, Edgar W.; and Goe, Steven J. "Evolution of a Strategy for the Retrieval of Cases in Longitudinal Survey Research." *Sociology and Social Research* 58 (1973):37-47.

National Opinion Research Center. Student Identification Pages (questionnaire). *High School and Beyond Project*. NCES Form 2409 -07, 1980.

Office of the Federal Register. *Code of Federal Regulations 45 Public Welfare Parts 1 to 99*. "Part 99—Privacy Rights of Parents and Students." Rev. October 1, 1979. Washington, D.C.: U.S. Government Printing Office, 1979.

Otto, Luther B.; Call, Vaughn, R.A.; and Spenner, Kenneth I. *Design for a Study of Entry into Careers*. Lexington, Mass.: Lexington Books, D.C. Heath, 1981.

Piliavin, Jane Allyn; and Piliavin, Irving M. "Effect of Blood on Reactions to a Victim." *Journal of Personality and Social Psychology* 23 (1972):353-361.

Piliavin, Irving M.; Rodin, Judith; and Piliavin, Jane Allyn. "Good Samaritanism: An Underground Phenomenon?" *Journal of Personality and Social Psychology* 13 (1969):289-299.

Rossi, Robert J.; Wise, Lauress L.; Williams, Kathleen L.; and Carrel, Kathleen S. *Methodology of the Project TALENT 11-Year Follow-up Study*. Palo Alto, Calif.: American Institutes for Research, 1976.

Schuman, Howard; and Johnson, Michael P. "Attitudes and Behavior." In *Annual Review of Sociology*, edited by Alex Inkeles, James Coleman, and Neil Smelser, pp. 161-207. Palo Alto, Calif.: Annual Reviews, 1976.

Schwartz, Shalom H. "Normative Influences on Altruism." In *Advances in Experimental Social Psychology*, edited by Leonard Berkowitz, pp. 222-275. New York: Academic Press, 1977.

Schwartz, Shalom H. "Temporal Instability as a Moderator of the Attitude-Behavior Relationship." *Journal of Personality and Social Psychology* 36 (1978):715-724.

Skeels, Harold M.; and Skodak, Marie. "Techniques for a High-Yield Follow-up Study in the Field." *Public Health Reports* 80 (1965):249-257.

Slocum, Walter L; Empey, L.T.; and Swanson, H.S. "Increasing Response to Questionnaires and Structured Interviews." *American Sociological Review* 21 (1956):221-225.

Steeh, Charlotte G. "Trends in Nonresponse Rates, 1952-1979." *Public Opinion Quarterly* 45 (1981):40-57.

Temme, Lloyd V. *The History and Methodology of the "The Adolescent Society" Follow-up Study.* Washington, D.C.: Bureau of Social Science Research, 1975.

U.S. Department of Commerce. Bureau of the Census. *Census of Population.* "Characteristics of the Population, Part 49: Washington," vol. 1, table 199. Washington, D.C.: U.S. Government Printing Office, 1970.

————. *Statistical Abstracts of the United States 1978.* 99th ed. Table 815. Washington, D.C.: U.S. Government Printing Office, 1978.

————. *Current Population Reports.* "Marital Status and Living Arrangements: March 1978," Series P-20, no. 338. Washington, D.C.: U.S. Government Printing Office, 1979.

————. *Current Population Reports.* "Geographical Mobility: March 1975 to March 1979," Series P-20, no. 353. Washington, D.C.: U.S. Government Printing Office, 1980*a*.

————. *Statistical Abstract of the United States 1980.* 101st ed. Table 1116. Washington, D.C.: U.S. Government Printing Office, 1980*b*.

U.S. Department of Health, Education, and Welfare. *First Marriages, United States, 1968-1976. Vital and Health Statistics.* Series 21, no. 35. Hyattsville, Md.: Office of Health Research, Statistics, and Technology, 1979.

Vigderhous, Gideon. "Scheduling Telephone Interviews: A Study of Seasonal Patterns." *Public Opinion Quarterly* 45 (1981):250-259.

Washington Post. "Pentagon Plans to Hunt Data on GIs in A-Tests." January 26, 1978.

————. "Army Unable to Locate Operation Smokey A-bomb Test Participants Who Have Likelihood of Developing Leukemia." February 15, 1978.

————. "U.S. Warning Links Illness to Asbestos." April 27, 1978.

Weeks, M.F.; Jones, B.L.; Folsom, Jr., R.E.; and Benrud, C.H. "Optimal Times to Contact Sample Households." *Public Opinion Quarterly* 44 (1980):101-114.

Wilcox, N. Elane. "Patient Follow-up: Procedures, Technics, and Devices for Improvement." *American Journal of Public Health* 55 (1965):1741-1756.

Willits, Fern K.; Crider, Donald M.; and Bealer, Robert C. *A Design and Assessment of Techniques for Locating Respondents in Longitudinal Sociological Studies.* University Park, Pa.: Pennsylvania State University, 1969.

————. *Twenty-Four Years Later: Migration and Success for a Panel of Rural Pennsylvanians.* Bulletin 831. University Park, Pa.: Pennsylvania State University, Agricultural Experiment Station, 1980.

Wise, Lauress L.; McLaughlin, Donald H.; and Steel, Lauri. *The Project TALENT Data Bank Handbook*. Palo Alto, Calif.: American Institutes for Research, 1977.

Zimbardo, Philip; and Ebbesen, Ebbe B. *Influencing Attitudes and Changing Behavior*. Reading, Mass.: Addison-Wesley, 1969.

Zimbardo, Philip; Ebbesen, Ebbe B.; and Maslach, Christina. *Influencing Attitudes and Changing Behavior*. 2nd ed. Reading, Mass.: Addison-Wesley, 1977.

Appendix A:
Address Return Cards
Used in Career
Development Study

Please...

Help make this study a success by filling out this form (both sides) and mailing it TODAY. A pre-addressed, postage-paid envelope is provided for your convenience.

1. What is George's current name and address? (Please print)

Name_____
         (first)   *(middle)*   *(last)*

Street_____

City_____State_____Zip_____

Phone number ( )_____

Form No. 999999   **Over**

2. Please indicate your full name and address on the lines below:

Name_____
         (first)   *(middle)*   *(last)*

Street_____   _____

City_____State_____Zip_____

Phone number ( )_____

1   **THANK YOU FOR YOUR HELP**

Address Return Card Sent to Parent

Please...

Help make this study a success by filling out this form (both sides) and mailing it **today.** A pre-addressed, postage-paid envelope is provided for your convenience.

1. Please indicate your full name and address on the lines below: *(Please print)*

Name_____
           (first)   *(middle)*   *(last)*

Street_____

City_____State_____Zip_____

Phone number (   )_____

Form No. 999999   **Over**

2. What is the current address for your parents?

Name_____
           (first)   *(middle)*   *(last)*

Street_____

City_____State_____Zip_____

Phone number (   )_____

5   **THANK YOU FOR YOUR HELP**

Address Return Card Sent to Respondent

Appendix B:
Envelopes Used
in Career Development
Study

CAREER DEVELOPMENT STUDY   999999
SOCIAL RESEARCH CENTER
WASHINGTON STATE UNIVERSITY
PULLMAN, WASHINGTON 99164

                                        Mr. George Parker
                                        7777 Charles Ave.
                                        Spokane, WA 99999

Outgoing Number 10 Envelope (reduced)

                        CAREER DEVELOPMENT STUDY
                        Social Research Center
                        Washington State University
                        Pullman, Washington 99164

Stamped Return Number 9 Envelope (reduced)

                                                            FIRST CLASS
                                                            PERMIT NO. 1
                                                            PULLMAN,
                                                            WASHINGTON

        Business Reply Mail
        NO POSTAGE STAMP NECESSARY IF MAILED IN THE UNITED STATES

        POSTAGE WILL BE PAID BY

        CAREER DEVELOPMENT STUDY
        Social Research Center
        Washington State University
        Pullman, Washington 99164

Business Reply Number 9 Envelope (reduced)

Appendix C:
Letters Sent to
Respondents in Career
Development Study

WASHINGTON STATE UNIVERSITY
PULLMAN, WASHINGTON 99164

CAREER DEVELOPMENT STUDY
SOCIAL RESEARCH CENTER

February 22, 1978

George Parker
7777 Charles Ave.
Spokane, WA 99999

Dear Mr. Parker:

In the spring of 1966 you were part of a very large study of the educational
and occupational goals of high school students. More than 7000 students from
the State of Washington reported on their educational and occupational plans.
At that time you, like your classmates, gave us an address where we might
be able to contact you in later years. We are now updating these addresses
and need to verify your current mailing address.

More than 10 years have passed since that study of high school students. We
are now studying the same group of people. We are finding out whether they
have been able to accomplish the educational and occupational goals they had
while in high school. Similar studies have been completed in the eastern
states, but as yet little is known about the career problems and experiences
of youth who attended Washington and western high schools. This scientific
study is designed to resolve some of the problems which concern parents who
are trying to help their sons and daughters prepare for the future.

We need your help in continuing this important research in which you took
park while at West Coast High School. We will be sending out information
about the continuing study and we want to forward it to you directly.

Enclosed is a card requesting verification of your current address and any
change in name since 1966. Please return it in the enclosed stamped envelope
so that we can proceed with the study.

If you have any questions about the study, contact Dr. James F. Short, Jr.,
Director, Social Research Center, Washington State University.

Thank you for your help.

Sincerely,

LUTHER B. OTTO, Ph.D.
Project Director

LBO:cas
Enclosures

First Reunion Letter

WASHINGTON STATE UNIVERSITY
PULLMAN, WASHINGTON 99164

CAREER DEVELOPMENT STUDY
SOCIAL RESEARCH CENTER

March 3, 1978

Ruth Thompson
8888 Elmwood Park
Spokane, WA 99999

Dear Ms. Thompson:

Last week we wrote asking for confirmation of your current
address. We want to send information explaining the continua-
tion of a study you participated in while attending West Coast
High School.

If you have already returned a card, accept our thanks for
your prompt assistance. If you have not returned it, simply
complete the enclosed card by providing your current address
and any name change. Please mail it today.

It is very important that we reach everyone who has been part
of this scientific study.

Thank you very much.

Sincerely,

LUTHER B. OTTO, Ph.D.
Project Director

LBO:cas
Enclosure

Second Reunion Letter

WASHINGTON STATE UNIVERSITY
PULLMAN, WASHINGTON 99164

CAREER DEVELOPMENT STUDY
SOCIAL RESEARCH CENTER

March 22, 1978

Terri Erickson
1112 Post Street
Tacoma, WA 98999

Dear Ms. Erickson:

About three weeks ago we wrote requesting confirmation of
your current address. We have not yet received a reply.

Approximately 10 years ago you were part of a long-term study
of Washington youth. We now need to make contact with you
again in order to update the information you provided us
while attending West Coast High School.

We ask for your help in verifying your current address and
any name change.

Please assist this important research by completing the
enclosed form. Mail the card today. A stamped, addressed
envelope is provided for your convenience. We await your
reply.

Thank you very much for your cooperation.

Cordially,

LUTHER B. OTTO, Ph.D.
Project Director

Third Reunion Letter

Appendix D:
Forms Used in
Telephone Tracking by
Career Development
Study

ID NUMBER _____

CURRENT PHONE DIRECTORY:

DIRECTORY ASSISTANCE OPERATOR:

CITY DIRECTORY:

OTHER LEADS:

Directory Search Record

NAME _____   PAGE _____ OF _____

1. WHO _____   BY _____

   WHEN _____/_____ _____   CITY _____
        month / day   time

   WHY _____   NUMBER (_____) _____

   RESULTS:

   _____

   _____

   _____

   _____

2. WHO _____   BY _____

   WHEN _____/_____ _____   CITY _____
        month / day   time

   WHY _____   NUMBER (_____) _____

   RESULTS:

   _____

   _____

   _____

   _____

3. WHO _____   BY _____

   WHEN _____/_____ _____   CITY _____
        month / day   time

   WHY _____   NUMBER (_____) _____

   RESULTS:

   _____

Telephone Tracking Record

LOCATE   ID# _____

NAME _____

ADDRESS _____

_____

PHONE _____

PARENT NAME _____

PARENT ADDRESS _____

_____

PHONE _____

DATE: _____

Tracking Address Record

Appendix E:
Information Request
Form Used in Career
Development Study

THREE FINAL THINGS . . . . . .

PAST -   - 1979 -   - FUTURE

Information Request Form (front cover)

FIRST: Some of the most important issues in education today center around the usefulness of high school courses and failing test scores. You provided us important information on these issues when you were in high school. Information is now needed about your high school coursework and test scores taken after the January 1966 survey was done. High schools will provide us this information if we receive a transcript request from you.

The transcript is the high school record that is normally sent to employers, schools and colleges when you apply for a job or college.

Please fill in the following for the **last high school** you attended.

PLEASE PRINT.

TO: _____
(name of last high school attended)

_____
(city)   (state)   (zip)

Please send a copy of my high school transcript and test scores to: Dr. Luther B. Otto
Career Development Study
Social Research Center
Washington State University
Pullman, Washington 99164

Date last attended high school: _____ 19 ____

Full name in 1966: _____

Birth date: _____   _____ 19 ____
            MONTH   DAY   YEAR

Signature: _____

Date: _____ 19 ____

SECOND: In another 10 or 15 years we may want to contact you again. Please give us the names and addresses of two people who would be able to help us locate you at that time (for example, brothers, sisters, friends, etc.).

1. NAME: _____

ADDRESS: _____

_____
city   state   zip

RELATIONSHIP: _____

2. NAME: _____

ADDRESS: _____

_____
city   state   zip

RELATIONSHIP: _____

IF MARRIED, Please PRINT your spouse's full name.

_____
(first)   (middle)   (last)

THIS INFORMATION WILL BE KEPT IN STRICT CONFIDENCE AND WILL ONLY BE USED IN FUTURE FOLLOW-UPS OF THE CAREER DEVELOPMENT STUDY.

(over)

Information Request Form (inside)

THIRD: HELP!

We have not been able to send information about this study to a few of your former classmates because we could not locate them. Every person in the study is important to us and cannot be replaced.

Please look over these names. Do you know where any of these people presently live or how we might get in touch with them or someone who knows where they are (for example brothers, sister, in-laws and the like)? Please note any information that may be helpful to us in locating them.

1966	**1966**
JUNIORS	**SENIORS**
Copper Charles	Hansen Patty
Johnson Cynthia	Jones Timothy
Larsen Penny	Olson Helen
Parker George	Smith John
	Thomas William
	Thompson Ruth

THANK YOU FOR YOUR HELP

PLEASE ENCLOSE THIS SHEET WITH THE QUESTIONNAIRE IN THE ENVELOPE WE HAVE PROVIDED FOR YOU

Information Request Form (back cover)

Indexes

Index of Authors

147

Index of Subjects

About the Authors

Vaughn R.A. Call received the Ph.D. from Washington State University in 1977. Since then he has been a postdoctoral Fellow and research associate with the Career Development Program. Dr. Call's research interests, presentations, and published articles focus on age at marriage and other major family events as these influence and are affected by occupational, educational, and military life-course events.

Luther B. Otto is director of the Career Development Program and director of the Research Division at the Boys Town Center. He has served as acting director of the Social Research Center at Washington State University. His research interests have focused on social psychology, stratification and mobility, and the sociology of education. Dr. Otto has published widely and has presented numerous professional papers on this research on the achievement process. He is a reviewer and editorial consultant for several professional journals and publishers. He is a regular consultant to private and public agencies in the field of education and work.

Kenneth I. Spenner received the Ph.D. in sociology from the University of Wisconsin-Madison in 1977. Since then he has been a postdoctoral Fellow and research associate with the Career Development Program. His research and published articles have been on social psychology and social stratification. His current research work centers on occupational characteristics, classification systems, and work careers.